About the editor

Tom Chivers is a writer, editor and promoter of poetry. Born 1983 in South London and educated at St Anne's College, Oxford, he is the author of *The Terrors* (Nine Arches Press, 2009) and *How To Build A City* (Salt Publishing, 2009). He previously edited and published *Generation Txt* (Penned in the Margins, 2006). He is associate editor of *Tears in the Fence* and was the first ever Poet in Residence at The Bishopsgate Institute.

City State
New London Poetry

Penned in the Margins
LONDON

PUBLISHED BY PENNED IN THE MARGINS
53 Arcadia Court, 45 Old Castle Street, London E1 7NY
www.pennedinthemargins.co.uk

First published 2009

Printed by Bell and Bain Ltd, Glasgow

ISBN
0-9553846-8-0
978-0-9553846-8-4

Contents

INTRODUCTION

For some time in the development of *City State*, my working subtitle was *The New London Poetry*. Anthologists make a habit of using that looming, numinous definite article, engineering provocative statements of fact. This is *it*. *The* Poetry. The rest is window-dressing.

But this anthology makes no such grand claim. There is no manifesto, no flag to raise, no team to join. The *The* was axed.

But *City State: New London Poetry* is not without shape, intent or agenda. The editor's role is always to inject his or her subjective taste into the book, not just sit back and wait for the work to roll in. What lies within represents my best subjective snap-shot of poetry as it is being practised in 2009 in London by a new generation of writers. I define this snap-shot as characteristic rather than representative; impressionistic rather than photographic. Crucially, *City State* aims to capture a diverse range of approaches to writing.

In the last five years I have perceived a real increase in poetry-related activity in London: new publishers and promoters are springing up everywhere (including online); there is greater ranger of work being written; poetry is engaging and reacting with other artforms and in performance. London is often described as a city of villages - a nostalgic notion propagated by estate agents and romantics, but one with some validity. In poetry terms, I would characterise the capital as a collection, not of villages, but of cultural hubs and hotspots. There is no single London poetry scene, and it's all the better for it. A scan through the biographies of the contributors to *City State* will reveal a matrix of familiar and unfamiliar names: independent publishers Salt, Tall Lighthouse, Flipped Eye and Veer; small magazines such as *The Wolf*, *Fuselit*, *Mimesis* and the gloriously photocopied *Rising*; important and dynamic creative writing courses at Queen Mary and those run by the influential poet Roddy Lumsden.

The numerous events and venues that host live poetry also play a crucial role in bringing writers together and providing platforms for performance and experimentation. Openned at The Foundry in Old Street has given London audiences the chance to witness appearances by a number of major UK and international avant-garde poets as well as nurturing a new generation of innovative writers. The Betsey Trotwood pub in Farringdon has become the unlikely home for a number of small, interconnected poetry communities (Broadcast, Tongue-Fu, The Shuffle and more). Promoters such as Poet in the City, Utter! and my own Penned in the Margins continue to work tirelessly to bring top-quality poetry to new audiences, alongside more established organisations such as Apples & Snakes.

It's no wonder so many young poets are drawn to the capital; of the contributors to this anthology fewer than half were born and raised in the city. London sucks in cultures and influences from elsewhere - from Wigan to Bombay - and then spits them back out in the form of poetry, music and art. For some the city plays a crucial role in their writing. The de facto poet laureate of the capital Iain Sinclair lurks ominously in the background of the work of many emerging London poets, myself included. For others, London is merely the place they've ended up, providing no more than urban backdrop to other personal or artistic concerns.

The poets featured in *City State* range in age from late teens to mid-thirties, in aesthetic from formalist to performance to post-avant and back again. Accordingly you will find what I hope to be an engaging and challenging mixture of potential and accomplishment that entertains, provokes debate and offers no easy answers.

Tom Chivers
East London, April 2009

City State

New London Poetry

We all live in the universe – this we should not forget, but aside from that, we each have a simpler and more definite address: a country, a city, a street, a building, an apartment. The presence of so precise an address is the criterion by which original poetry is distinguished from the pretentious and the artificial.

Samuil Marshak

A Milken Bud

Of all the things that were inside me
she is the part I miss the most. I remember:
through the black flashes and the sun-lit green,
I saw my flesh come away with the sand.
A surge unfastened my stomach,
the skin gently over-turned and the child
went away with wave. The last tissue
of my breast stuttered and I saw what I thought
was a strange white fish; only a milken bud
curdled in the nipple.

No, I was never a mother; I never brought to term
a lit cluster of dividing eggs, thriving like bulbs
and streaming behind me, like the proud amphibious
matriarchs hatching their young in my hip bone.

I would have taken her for night walks.
I would have shown her the wonder of streetlights
pouring forth cascades of orange water.
Or the blue that bleeds brown that is the London sky

at dusk. Chips and vinegar. I still imagine her
making an O with her lips, blowing at the hot
and pungent chip that burns her tongue,
and her warm breath escaping.

You who'd put a hammer in my head:
I'd have suckled that child headless.
Put a boot in my face: I'd have held her faceless.
I'd have walked her home with my
gashed eye weeping.

F12

I have pared around your wrists with light.
I will always have the deep crease in your thumb
your cupped & faceless hands around
my limbless waist. My green skin against
your blue skin

transposed & re-hung. You with your eyes closed on the Circle
Line into you with the deep crease around your mouth into you
with the shadow of St. Paul's obscuring you into a woman sipping
into a woman stepping from a bus into the wine-chalk street.

Twice; I am behind a lens, behind an eye; again, behind a skull,
behind a brain, behind a mind; my view is ragged. The frame is
torn. All those people who made the world magic are gone.
Grown. I'm not ready for the flesh to double

& double. I end the alphabet at U. I point, I click, I catch
the second when your head was turned, or when a dog leapt from
a puddle at a bird. I shutter the world in two; your two hands
separate from you.

Between this world and the next hour I will gaze at you &
you & you. I am behind the eye that froze you feeling a dasheen.
I am behind the gloss, behind the print, behind the page.
Behind the blunt lens that cut you out and kept you.

I am cracked soap,
melting in the bath.
Scum on the taps.
I undress and put one foot in.
Swole ankle changes in the water.
Gets slim. Toes get bubbles.
Then lower myself in.
Pray for powercut.
THEN it will be just me
And sound of water, and it
running in my eyes.
(HEAR two boy cursing as they pass)
Just scrub the skin,
Armpit, neck, ear.
Clean everything.
The mirror steams.
I lift my hand to it —
Just some colour on glass.

A Love Song

Long before we tie the knot, Divorce moves in.
He sits on the naughty step, patting his knees.

Crowned in towel, I step out the shower
and he's there, handing me a raffle ticket.

He plays kick-about with the neighbourhood kids,
chalks crosses on their doors and buys them Big Macs.

Socking his fist into the bowl of his hat,
he'd kicked the gate wide, that sunny day in Leeds.

My mum was incredulous, "she's only ten,
she can't possibly have made contact with you."

He clocked my young face and handed me his card.
'Call me when you fall in love, I'm here to help.'

Perhaps he smelt something in my pheromones,
a cynicism rising from my milk-teeth.

With gum, he stuck notes on Valentine's flowers:
tiny life-letters in factual grey ink.

The future cut two keys for a new couple.
On my twenty-first, Divorce took the spare room.

He loves to breathe down the spout of the kettle,
make our morning coffee taste mature and sad.

He waits by the car, slowing tapping Tic-tacs
down his throat. We've thought about stabbing him,

but he's such a talented calligrapher:
our wedding invitations look posh as pearl.

He bought us this novelty fridge-magnet set,
a naked doll with stick-on wedding dresses.

Divorce and I sometimes sit in the kitchen,
chucking odd magnetic outfits at the fridge.

He does the cooking, guarding over the soup,
dipping his ladle like a spectral butler.

He picks me daisies, makes me mix-tapes, whispers
'call me D,' next thing he'll be lifting the veil.

After the honeymoon, we'll do up the loft,
give Divorce his own studio apartment.

We must keep him sweet, my fiancé agrees,
look him in the eye, subtly hide matches,

remember we've an arsonist in the house.
The neighbours think we're crazy, pampering him

like a treasured child, warming his freezing feet,
but we sing Divorce to sleep with long love songs.

Our Infidelity

Swans were dying in the street, taxis
swerving to avoid their dainty
carcasses and I was sloshing wine
in a badly-lit restaurant with a candle,
an ache between my legs and a crack
in the window for the guilt.

This infidelity of ours was so steaming hot
the waitresses were dropping plates, running
their fingers under the cold tap, and swans
- as I said – were exploding by the river.

We didn't need to kiss: the sky had already
started burning, people screaming naked
in gasoline-coats through the Christmas lights,
a vicar on a soap-box, somewhere, judging
our souls and a grubby child – an orphan probably –
singing 'where is love? Is it underneath the willow-tree?'

There weren't any willow-trees by then,
just smoking stumps and charred mittens
hanging on the air. But you were so beautiful,
it almost didn't matter that a car crashed
every time you smiled. I could almost block out
the sound of sirens and apocalyptic distress.

At the bus stop, I told you - telepathically –
it wasn't our fault: the dead swans,
the seething man-holes, the heat. Tomorrow
giant watering-cans will drip from cranes
into our respective gardens where our respective
partners will be dancing, wet with innocence.

Last Tuesday

I miss my Tuesday so much. I had a Tuesday
today, but it wasn't the same. It tasted funny.
There were signs it had already been opened.
The seal was broken. Someone had poisoned it
with Wednesday-juice. In fact, I think today
was actually Wednesday, but the government
was trying to pass it off as Tuesday by putting
my tennis lesson back a day, rearranging the
tea-towels. I sent a letter to MI5 and CIA
and the rest. I know they have my Tuesday.
They're keeping it for experiments because it
was so freakishly happy. I was smiling in my
sleep when two men in body-sized black socks
stole it from my bedside table. It was here.
It was right here. But when I woke up, it was
gone. Their Wednesday stole my Tuesday.
Their frigging totalitarian cloud-humped shit-
swallower of a Wednesday stole my innocent
Tuesday. And now it's just getting ridiculous:
the days change every week, it's like an avalanche.
As soon as I start to get the hang of a day, learn
the corridors, find my locker-key, the bell goes
and suddenly it's Thursday, or Friday, but not
last Friday or Thursday, oh no, these are different
ones, with knees-caps like pustules, gangly eyes:
you never know which way they'll lunge.

In the Lost Property Office, I held up the queue.
It's greenish, I told the attendant, with a mouth
that opens to a courtyard. But they only had a box
of wild Fridays some lads had misplaced in Thailand.
(I took a couple of those, for the pain.) Then I
gave up. I ignored the days, and they ignored me.
I drank Red Bull in the ruins of monasteries,
flicking through calendars of digitally-enhanced dead
people: Gene Kelly downloading a remix of
'Singing in the Rain' on his slim-line Apple Mac.
No one gives a damn about time anymore. Happy hour
lasts all afternoon. You can put a hat on a corpse
and send it to work. You can bury a baby.

Hip counsellors in retro tweed jackets keep
telling me to look ahead. There'll be other Tuesdays
to enjoy, they say, new Tuesday pastures. It's a lie.
I found my Tuesday in someone else's bed.
Its chops were caked in velvet gel, and its voice
had corrupted. It pretended to be a Saturday,
but I could see myself reflected in its eyes, a younger
me, tooting the breeze with a plastic trombone.
"I'm sorry," said my Tuesday, pulling its hand out
of a woman, "I didn't mean to let you down, but
I couldn't stay perfect forever, you were suffocating me.
Even sacred memories need to get their rocks off."

To Not Drinking on Wall Street

to not drinking on Wall Street I have never been
to Wall Street it is a synecdoche as I am thinking
about not drinking and saving money the screen
is a colourful mass of esoteric maths and gloom I'm not drinking
while I write because of money and because in Polish
you telephone 'to' someone and people are 'on' a picture
and this is no reason to turn me to drink but I want the polish
of a flamboyant metaphor that booze gives its tincture
it is so cold here - touch a car with your bare fist
and it'll likely stick or break something smash!
you can't win wheel away from that kind of fast
thinking and you'll find it's the drink just a splash
of it and wow you've been a silly boy little man!
and on Wall Street the money is ouf bosh down the pan

And a Pan is a Funny Thing to Gong

and a pan is a funny thing to gong the rhyme on there
Pan is what all unknown men are called
in Poland over the dill in the supermarket they stare
in a Slavonic deadpan of the eyes which would scald
if they weren't so cold and occasionally beautiful
I concede happily no problem does Pan know how much
this gaunt little white onion is? imagine fields full
of lutes pot-bellied dancing vats of such
fragrant liquor juniper honey and bison grass
or imagine poured concrete fields with the glass
layer of hoarfrost the burning dustbin the trio
of abandoned shoes (matching! left right left!) the slow
movement of a very low sun tries to climb
beyond dawn or dusk does Pan have the time?

Beyond Dusk or Dawn by Daylight

beyond dusk or dawn (by daylight or streetlight)
I wouldn't hang about on Camberwell Green
unless for a drink which I do do do you? right
right you are don't it isn't true no not clean
not green nor well and no camber to speak of until
you've been drinking or other things we won't speak
of you do not call 'to' anyone laughably shrill
in the engine room burr at the dead of the week
(that is Monday thru Sunday) nobody is 'on'
the picture but some are on fire on heat on things
which are worse and a gaunt little white onion
of a man with his head and arms in adidas slings
an indictment your way and observes that the green
is yellow and brown like a bruise and it always has been.

I Took a Gaunt Little

I took a gaunt little pan of white onions from
Camberwell Green to here to Wall Street punched
my ticket on the tram watched the validator hum
when its teeth sunk in that's the ticket not bunched
up like a messy fiver or it won't fit in or be valid
got to pierce the queen's nose (she's 'on' the note
but not on the picture) but in Poland it's a pallid
BILET and inordinate consonants up high in the throat
and the well-aligned teeth and don't drink on the tram
with my Capricorn feet like Ugg boots with claws
my Capricious beard black white ginger snap straws
and its not alopecia doctor in my efforts to cram
every hue in I aliment with liquor and slap
on my maquillage horns nestle under my cap

When Pan the Only Dead God Lost

when Pan the only dead god lost his long life
savings and took solace in his mortal position
started drinking cursing Wall Street took a breadknife
to Camberwell Green with a bag of those onions
little gaunt white bought a bag of Camberwell Green
and told himself the most Capricious joke
(look, I'm dead!) took out his pipe from the skein
of his crosshatched loins had an Arcadian smoke
he devised a new cogito fit for his state
it was ravenous drinking not thinking the first antic
verb really he was 'on' Camberwell Green far too alone
to imagine a field not Arcadian lush not a slick
of poured concrete does Pan have to moan
like a goat with his sibilants spittling the screen
in panic from Wall Street to Camberwell Green?

SIDDHARTHA BOSE

Shoreditch Serenade

She blinks—
I was burned outta the Royal Oak, closing time.
I glimpsed a crack in the glass, which grew to
        Spider legs.
Winter buds waited for springsap,
        Dressed like Chinese lanterns.

                Hanging from branches.

Last night, my friend, we made the end of a
Story—as usual, you were late. I
Held my cell like a
        Crucifix to watch you
                Stumble towards me in the
                        Coal of a London street.

        ~

He thinks—
I'm not sure. Never am.

I drink to be animal.

At home in a psssoaked alley off Kingsland Road, I
Clock a rubbersmell pinot grigio, jiving to
      Bombay underground.

To build faith, I flagellate my
      Bloodliver, a believer on Muharram.
            God will fasten my plea,
                  Chainspike my flesh-hide.

I whistle, crippling to meet you on Columbia Road.

    ~

She hones —
I hurled you
      Into my arms, the
            Cat in my voice a queen.

You, ever in reserve, shied.

Around us, East London took effect —

      A Pole, two Sicilians, married, two Greeks drinking Cobra
                              beers,
          Fang in hand, Emily the scouse violinist, a German
                           who
         Thought Berlin too small.

As we floated like
                    Bottletops, scrap-paper, haymoss,
Towards the estuary where Bethnal Green meets Brick Lane, I
                    Felt I'd lost my wallet.

                    I, artisan.

                    ~

He groans —
You order me, again, to
                    Glen them to a bar where two summers ago Naphtali
                                        Spun me in axes.
(You'll be there in a minute, you say.)

I lead your followers past bagel shops, hookah bars, offlicence
                                                            glory,
                    Cops prowling, the becoming dinosaur of the overhead rail,
                                                            the
                                        Bombed remains of
                                        Cheap vinyl, soggy crêpes, torn jeans, pillpoppers.

                                        I am a helicopter.

                    ~

She streaks —
Cityboys them fucked off.
As I walked towards you, ma money in ma pocket, through

Graffitishocked streets, colours
      Bled me with the damp of a morning star.

Squatters them sclattered in the
      Dungeon of a broken house, peeled windows.

Some paint on scorpio bodies. Others hiss on cheap blow.
      My eyes trance in redn'green shapes.

   ~

He seeks —
Hood of speed makes way in the bar —
      Costume crunched, mascara masked, bass heavy
      Ballsweat tinge of fahrenheit.
         Junkheads dance like coins tossed.

Russian at the crystal counter, studying film, winks through a
                           funnel.
Athenian blathers on opera.
I shade my way to the plastic of the street, where I miss the Punjabi
                          bouncer who
      Spoke in cricket.

A musician, close from Chicago,
      Beat-boxes me to movement 'n' sound. A
      Mama from Sao Paolo
         Souls to rhythm. A
      Dread-man looking like a lost friend, calls her posh,

Sings like it is, showing
Me his needles.

You emerge, glow from dew.
Your breasts are temples.

~

She grooves —
Gin 'n' tonic fought me off, shook me solid. I
Spoke of Ghatak, hoped you'd understand. You
Dropped on your back, flailed like an
Alligator's tail. I
Balked, my lips forming soot.

Our friends grew ghosts on their backs. A
Vomit of people gathered on the road. The
Spanish, who lock the afterhours scenes,
Ritualed in fluorescence, deep in Commercial Street.

I motioned us — all of us —
Back to my den, a lion.

~

He hooves —
On your bed, I watch Emily play with Grotowski with
Crackedglass tooth. He no let her go, and she
Sinks in his shipsoil. They

Fall on tiles, solving politics.

Sao Paolo's husband calls her a black cab back to Chancery
                                                    Lane.
Chicagoman takes Hackney Wick by storm.

I tell you my life is a Lou Reed song.

I carve it out for you, a turkey.
I make an offering, in pollen.

            ~

She grins —
They went, you stayed,
            Proud.

Sun slivered to the room, I watched the
            Shyness bloom you.

I gave balloons, pinked you to health.
Washed you in stars.
Held you strong as cradle.
                Milked you to leave.
        I'll see you again, I oceaned, my
 Teeth heavy with lead.

            ~

He sins —
Overhead, sky forms a light-wedge.
Construction cranes in the distance
      Gleam like flamingos. On Fashion Street, orange sun, sari-
                     red clouds
         Roll towards me in four horsemen. I hear
            Thunder lift like elephants. A woman in
                 veil
               Slits towards me, her eyes cry as
                 knives.
                 She keels herself, kneel in
                 chin, summoning
                 God in trousers.

I am sane in tortured times.
         I dream your salt.
                 You are gone.

The Islanders

The islanders we met were digital natives;
bronzed and nubile, their ankles garlanded
with flash drives fashioned from conch-shells.

They spoke an elevated form of hypertext,
interspersed with Java: a dialect
I recognised as coded status updates.

At dusk they danced a ritual waltz,
the men intoning Windows logoff
as the sun passed over the horizon

and the elders tuned into bootleg Wifi signals,
invoked the souls of obsolete technology,
ancestral operating systems that were here

when the land was new. Early settlers
taught them how to farm, to tend the land,
keep imported Tamagochi as livestock.

The women showed us how they worked
the pulpy Sega plant into a pixelated broth,
set their hair with braided power leads.

The youth assigned us island names:
I was 'Sonic' – on account, they said,
of my speed in the hunt when we tracked

the wild software through the jungle
to the centre of the island
where the outcasts lived, those

who'd given up the old ways,
switched their mobiles off,
refused to check their emails,

traded silicon chips for rifles, set off
on merchant ships for distant lands
beyond the range of gods and elders.

When one year passed, I took an island wife
compatible to me, installed her in a makeshift
hut with views over the bay. Her Firewall

was good, but I was unrelenting. I thought
it was a thing like love, but she insisted
I just had the caps lock on.

Poem as bullet

A typographic rukus interrupts
their dense arrangement of wires;
language for its own sake was
alone on top of a cold building.

Steel performs a shedding of skin
in reverse. The snake creeps back
inside. In truth, the whole metropolis
is bleeding from the guts and gums.

To order space when we cannot even
tell the time – to me, that seems absurd.

Some scrag in a poncho screaming
How's your father? to a rookery of

knaves who've missed the deadline,
press execute and drop. The signal

to advance arrives, but through a process
of erasure, ritualised in stocks, fails to

register; they slump. Soon it will be 2010.
Incendiary devices are improvised

from the rotting shells of dead poets.

Speaking of the Dead

Entrances

Unsure to whom to speak
we linger in the hallway,
padding the carpet with our heavy feet.

Inside, encrypted versions of our former selves
perform the perfect soufflé.

I levitate the hat-stand.
In theory I could leave,
but what comes out is like a language
only twisted, not our own.
We try to understand in objects:
spoons, cups, unlocked doors.
"No-one listens," we complain,
log on to check our mail
to find that all accounts are hacked,
avatars we spent ten years maintaining
now just floating icons on dead-end servers.

We shuffle at the window in the hall.
The city's trying to get in.
A cloud of brick-dust implicates the past;
the sound of engines stalling.

"THIS is not a political act," I manage,
but the blind men have already turned away.

Dreams

At the dead centre of a dream
where X marks the spot
the light switched off, or would have;
at the end of the garden
where the wild badger stirs
in his sett and the alley,
damp with fox, hexed
by another world's junk,
leads out to the city
and back to the pier
stretched from a shore and
going nowhere. The waves are big,
like Hokusai's *Great Wave off Kanagawa*,
a feat of weight and water
turning itself over itself,
and the pier is a ladder that's fallen
and so is the dream
and everything
and this.

Exits

We moved through the place like
ghosts, really, wearing oversized coats,
the petrified stares of stuffed mammals
as masks. We crept backstage,
rearranged the things we thought
would be noticed: props on a table,
cosmetics, a wig. I smelt the pigeons
rustling in the rafters, a puff of feathers.

The Hall fell silent. Or rather, we listened
to the silence that was already there
in the worlds we'd built in miniature,
the scheduled exits and the walk-on parts
who shift clumsily in velvet
as Lord such-and-such.

The darkness gave way;
all around us was light;
we could see the bones in our hands
and the way they were fixed,
and the cue, when it came,
was clearer than that;
and I knew what to do
and I did it, not
with the snarl of a fox –
like a bird, released,
that was caught in a roof.

Homework

We're falling for each other like kids on buses,
waiting for the heady curve of Waterloo

to hit the upper deck with rounded roads
so we can tumble chest-first into one another

and call it a mistake. That's fine, my love –
but though you can fight me like homework,

sit at the table and scream yourself to sleep,
I'll still be here in the morning, open, undone,

and you'll have to take me in with you,
so think of an excuse.

To the man reading *Country Walks* on the Central Line

Yes, I too have stretched myself to this;
concrete has no give and I need to feel
the ground beneath me soft as cereal
under boots you could kill a man with.
In this gutted parkland, stripped, lobotomised
until you would think that this is where
electricity actually comes from, I too miss the scent
of shit and hillsides, long to skin my palms
on strips of bark, and can't remember when
I tasted dirt beneath my bitten nails.
I too feel my spine knot at the sound
of strangers chewing or kissing on the tube;
I too prefer the smell of rotting lamb,
skull caved and fly-spotted, pushed to the edge
of a field by its fatalistic mother,
to the tang of aftershave in a warm carriage.
Take my hand. We'll run these escalators out
to a spot where the leaves split from the trees
like mercury from a dropped thermometer;
we'll roll down hills until our hips and ribs
are collages of bruises and blood. See, our feet
nearly touch and we're wearing similar shoes.
No, there is no need to shift in your seat,
or turn to the girl on your left who is leafing
through property guides, her hand on your hand.

The Lasting Dead

The Hunterian Museum, Royal College of Surgeons, Lincoln's Inn Fields, WC2

The men in here have skin that peels away
from the root of the face, like a climbing harelip,
muscles strung out into strips of wound,
fat pumped with pigment. Some rest in their bells,
soaked in formaldehyde, whitened by acid
to something more like marble. Some are dry

and hang among the open guts of girls
who died whilst giving birth, their abdomens
side by side with a shining chunk of skull
belonging to a four year old. Her skin
and eyelashes and hair intact, she seems
to be asleep, dreaming of the rest of her.

The skeleton of flesh that firmed to bone
and fused its owner shut like a rusted door
has stayed together through the century –
through blasts of war, when the building's front
was blown away as neatly as the face
of the soldier sketched along the upstairs wall.

To have come across the rubble of these rooms,
have reached beneath, found slices of corpse,
and, recognising each, rebuilt the place

out of the lasting dead. To be their surgeon,
to blindly lift the skin, touch threads beneath,
and still to know exactly where you are.

I will use my years of northern weather

wisely, watch the greyscale of buildings and sky,
checking to see how they change with each day.
I will sit at the edge of a Shoreditch squat,
gazing as the ceiling sifts plaster on dancers
and ricketing hail starts to bludgeon the place,
then lean on my lover, say *Parties like this*
were all over West Yorkshire. When rainstorms strike,
with acres of sea crashing into the streets,
I will turn up my jacket against the commotion
and laugh in my collar of summers I knew –
June days when rain came from a hot blue sky,
when my shoes were so wet for so long they grew mould,
and how I never wore a coat outside.
In basement bars, as thunder spills the drinks,
I will turn to a crowd of shivering accountants
and make them sick with laughter by sharing the months
I spent as the lousiest waiter in Lancashire
in that drab hillside canteen, my windswept hair
and chapped lips stopping customers complaining;
when the barman refreshes my gin at a blink
I will place my dry hand on an actuary's knee
and tell him the secrets of how I survived
that night the tiles all cut loose from my house.
When seconds of sunshine explode on Oxford Street
I will grab for a towel in the nearest store,
fling it onto the pavement, or between standstill cars

and shout *You never know* as I sit down.
I will grow shiny and pink in seconds, start to itch,
then think of all the things I need to do.
I will talk to people on buses, call them *love*
even when they hate me, and my reputation
will come to creep in front of me with flags
until I am not just the talk of the Jubilee Walk,
but a monument, a living statue not expecting change.
I will think to myself, as the sun shrinks and fades,
of the futures I planned during winters where days
were night-times with six hour shifts for the light:
the years of sharp rent and the weekends alone,
the gunshots, the tube times, the shifting careers,
the streets stretching miles, with the rich at their edges.
When urban sophisticates scratch down my door
and bribe me, their cocktails and furs and cigars,
to tell them just how I got through it unscathed,
I will look at their backdrop, the city's collapse,
and say, *I used my years of northern weather*.

ALEX DAVIES

In which the Mad Dean climbs the dome of St Paul's

A pocketwatch tale from the scume ridden cobblepot penny dreadfuls of ye olde England. Behold a ramshackle public house, populated by sideburns and neckerchiefs. Inside, The Beast rakes at a sylla(bub) with his indestructible claws, tears in his handkerchiefs, devilish pig-fighting scars on his face and hands cannot be healed by his choleric gut. Cut to: one side of one street, the Dean marches past the gaslight with two leather satchels griped with bibles, half a tonne of King James's and a gross of Tyndale. Cut to: one side of the other street, William Terriss stops and considers the raven. When the raven pauses also, to consider him, he moves on. Cut to: the center of the two streets, in the cowboy dust and midnight dusk, § Doffed Cap immolates at a crossroads and the cognoscenti spark up roll ups off his charring corpse. Someone drops a one-armed bandit on a printing press, tickling Gutenberg's dovetailed beard like a harem shuffle, memoirs condensed in oolite and clay. The Cap's indestructible shield is melting over his arm, an impossible machine; as he burns, The Beast chokes on the Pantone fumes, entirely of the government's devising. Cut to: an Indian restaurant, opposite the pub, on the other side of the other street: The Professor separates a

Lamb Rogan Josh into two equal portions on his plate and glowers at it. Atop the dome, the climbéd Dean peals. Cut to: Mister city policemen sitting pretty little policeman in Saville rows, see how they run like pigs from a gun to the mise en scène of the crying. Two biros taped together can draw a river on a reporter's notebook, or two synchronised tapeworms, or superstrings, quantum filaments, the spooling conundrum, hansom cabs and deerstalkers, dainty feet on the flint cobblestones, some kind of bony corbomite maneuever: floating Da Vinci helicopters held by children dogfighting on the gulf. There's seven ancient pawn shops beside the bank, and seven aching deities and they want to know: when the Lion moves why does it howls and bite at thin air? The Beast snatches at the old man's cane, but his claws have turned to twigs and he gets splinters in his eyes. Cut to: a screever, screaming: 'Our idols idols are sculpted from the finest recycled materials.' Peel the rancid Intel sticker from the horse's hoof with a sonic screwdriver. The stone on which the city fails lies beneath a bank, caged in smog. If Brutus knew of the fate of the heart of the city, he would have ferried posterity elsewhere. The cage rattles, fermented to the heart of abuse. Beyond the indictment of successive generations, a pink goo filters through the detritus of London's arterial motives, with Bazelgette's intestines distended by aborted pig foetuses and swine teeth. A cyclops splashes his way through polished turds and discarded fighter jets, the emblem threatening to scythe the small of his back. 11 years previous was the speech of a radical fundamentalist and his performance of an entombed heart bypass (such was his head shaped) taped, old-style, on a tape, to exclusion of digital media destroyed since inception of nuclear dosage. On tape, with Velcro beard and musk tones, the fundamentalist proclaims the end of civilized London. It is a moment of fire, the initiation of proclivities fielded amongst terrorists for the embellishment of the supposedly free world, a call to arms for firebombing of Nelson's column, a syphilitic flaming rash gathering around the lions that roar stone in pain, unable to avoid piercing bullets of AK47s, the stirring of the Thames with high explosives, in death the sky bloated, crowds scattering in lieu of the underarm stench settling over the high ground. The Dean, lynched by self-perpetuating guilt, a state of thought bartering thought for feeling, climbéd the spire of the cathedral a day seven years post-transaction, the heady boudoir inside culminating in furious group masturbation, the height of society, a debauched debacle with convoluted plans to reclaim the sanity of the City. Above the droning bugles and bagpipes lilting on the rising smoke, the accumulation of fat men's cigars punched through St. Paul's dome. The Dean clutches the spear and humps his grievances away on the crucifix, weeping like a castrato, steel cable the river the day before the bomb hit Big Ben and the clock imploded, time and its markings fell on the ants of the city and stabbed and squashed them, glass shards ripping eyes in half, golden debris crushing the heads of children, and the unfortunate gentlemen who received a second hand through the chest, which, quite deliciously for the soon-to-gather media, stopped his heart ticking.

Area Sneaks

We may watch the tower of London crumble and be glad, bridge stuck yawning under awnings manufacturing Dodger marrow, artful yelping the first taste of past glories, churning yak, spawning riverside misery, the stench of stale beer rising through the Proud galleries. 'Dickensian whores to a man,' he says, 'Ruffles, Priggers, Swaddlers, Swig-Men, Strowlers, Dommerers, Glimmerers, Bully-Huffs, Bugger-Nabbers, Rum-Bubbers, Bung-Nippers, Mumpers, Capperdogeons and Tatmongers,' he says. 'And what of us?' Dribbling fiscal warnings on to comics, he empties holy water into a shopping cart, pop bottles in spitfires, a steel grub gorging on the fin de siècle Blitz, a Nazi little surprise. Those vaudevillians in limelight, inhaling mustard gas, too old men two step up. Us now use inhalers, the mustard gas, no wish to suck ourselves, stay down, cowered, wooden lads Fear splinters, pickpocket joists tear the skin where flies plant eggs and metal rusts. So we row the Queen into the Thames, the river itself, armed with empty pockets, for glorious We are the last night of the Proms. The tube-worm, obese, detonates, circulates cholera as its mouths clamps closed-swallows the Royal Mint. Pantone air chokes choleric consumptives into random bursts of defiance, Queen Mary croaks SOS and the crowd disperses. He reaches up and through the bars below the bank, an area sneak with a hollowed-out index finger, touching the stone writing in blood, red blood.

Clubbing

It begins with shackling necklaces across throats:
the distorted custom of wearing amulets to battle,
talismans to war; we are new hunters, wear jeans

for camouflage, clutch mobile phones like spears,
journey to the village/town/city square, meet
the rest of the tribe, mostly in short skirts, armed

with stilettos, armoured by Chanel. Dusk thickens,
the customary bickering between us commences
through the jungle vines of power lines/stampede

of zebra crossings/night growth of streets bustling,
our ritual is natural, till the traders come. Greater
armed, they divide with such ease that most of us

are taken. Those who resist are swayed by liquor
deals, sailed to darkness where the master spins
a tune not our own. We move stiffly to it as minds

force indifference, but spines have a preference
for drums. Rage building, we make our melody,
fight to find our feet until the master tries to mix

our movement with his song… but the rhythm is
uneven and the tempo, wrong. Against its waves,
we raise voices in anger, fists in protest, dancers

in the tide, militant against the music, a million
men marching through seas. But we still know
how to cross water; the ocean holds our bones,

explains our way of navigating past bouncers
like breeze into night's air, where clouds pass
like dark ships and find us beached, benched

with parched lips, loose-limbed and looking
to light. Now, the best thing about clubbing
is not this, or the struggle to make hips sway

just so, not the need to charge cloakrooms
as if through underground railroads. No.
Best thing about clubbing is the feeling

of freedom on the ride home.

GuerillaGardenWritingPoem

The mouth of the city is tongued with tar,
its glands gutter saliva, teeth chatter in rail
clatter, throat echoes car horns and tyres
screech, forging new language: a brick city,
smoke-speak of stainless steel consonants
and suffocated vowels. These are trees and
shrubbery, the clustered fauna battling all
hours, staccato staggered through streets.

Meet Rich and Eleanor on Brabourn Grove
as he wrestles her wheelbarrow over cobble-
stones to the traffic island by Kitto Road
where this night, coloured a turquoise-grit,
cathedral-quiet and saintly, makes prayer
of their whispers and ritual of their work:
bent over, clear rubble, cut weed and plant.

But more than seeds are sown here. You
can tell by his tender pat on tended patch;
the soft cuff to a boy's head - first day to
school, by how they rest with parental pride
against stone walls, huff into winter's cold,
press faces together as though tulips might
stem from two lips, gather spades, forks,
weeds and go. Rich wheelbarrows back to
Eleanor's as vowels flower or flowers vowel

through smoke-speak, soil softens, the city
drenched with new language, thrills and
the drains are drunk with dreams.

The sky sways on the safe side of tipsy
and it's all together an alien time of half
life and hope, an after-fight of gentle fog
and city smog, where debris of dew drips
to this narrative of progress, this city tale;
this story is my story, this vista my song.

I cluster in the quiet, stack against steel
seek islands, hope, and a pen to sow with.

Corinne Bailey Rae

First time I hear Corinne Bailey Rae, I feel like
her voice would fit the first song post-apocalypse.
It's gentle, momentous, comes heralding a new age,
slow, as if through burning clouds, drifting past the
carbon nonsense sleepily, a humble thing weeping
for beauty, creeping into time.

Try to speak of this passing to a friend who shrugs:
Dude just press rewind, listen again. I grumble,
comply, but he missed the point.

And maybe he should have.

Maybe for him, her voice isn't sky-borne or drifting.
Instead, a captured clasp of earth spirit, an orchid
of the valley or some kindred of hymns. For music
comprehension is a varied thing; as words only
grasp at meaning, chords try to clasp mood -
it calls interpretation and all answers are true.

The hi-fi plays this newly favoured tune,
speakers spawn sound waves. I climb baselines
like ladders, notes like rungs, climb till nestled,
centering the song, waft through window now wood,
keys and wings, a human amplifier audio colouring
the wind. Internalising, I am the song in all things,

the guitarist's fingertips pressed against nylon,
the gentle roar of a drum, a tired lion unwinding
in the Serengeti of strings. The baseline dwindles,
song fades, and dropped noise naked, barefooted,
off-beat, note how quiet, how still lies the street.

No rival music. No bullying beat. Not the mischief
magic of children scurrying, whatever else moves
does so discreet. It's a tumbleweed from a Texan
desert and this street holds guns and outlaws,
how the Wild West way fits the clear morning!

I climb through the window, pull the blinds shut
save a light beam that tingles, touching corners,
growing bold; by its brightness, a pattern unfolds.

The beam hits a tumbled glass and scatters:
glass plays prism, a rainbow pallet splatters,
colours come into their own:

Red rides an apple, bleeds into a burning
candle's orange glow, wax drips onto a copy
of *Othello*, the yellow'd paper greens where
blue ink stains, fades to a dusty indigo,
rests on a violet folder.

This harmonious, violent, accidental rainbow
hits a mirror, smatters across the room, sends
a thousand things twinkling in the summer gloom.

A confined borealis blinks: sinks into the swirl and
soft madness of a still warm duvet, where the ghost
of sleep rises to meet the ghost of music; entwines
in the sparse sparkle.

Even the worn footpaths in the carpet
look like crop circles.

And a natural mystic fills the air.

In this jigsaw puzzle devised by one far diviner
than I, I am the piece where the mountain peak
meets the sky; the silence amplifying skin prism
reforming the light, who fits within the ceiling,
blue walls and floor boards.

I wonder, if in someplace other,
one mile from here, similar room, similar clutter,
maybe a browner shade of blue, someone kneels:
head in the clouds, body in a valley of hymns,
listens to Corinne's captured clasped spirit
and wonders about fitting in?

Summer. Ha!

Diagonals from the sky
fatly crosshatched
by wet winners of
gravity v surface tension
battles at roof corners.
Uh uh uh uh
impolite insistence
of umbrella edges.
July in London.
I am the confluence
of three waters.
Swooshing tyres –
a skirtwards parabola.
Make that four.

Preset 3

digital birdsong
is great
it's like
I'm in
the countryside
except that
yellow streetlight
bleeds through
fusty curtains
made by
someone's gran

kids with
muscly dogs
outshriek sirens
but really
you know
it's not
too bad
so turn
it up
and shut
your eyes

Rollerblading in theory and practice

I am standing tall, knees softly bent and feet shoulder-width apart.

About 40% of my body is protected by a plastic exoskeleton. My arms are slightly out in front, palms downwards as if pushing an imaginary shopping trolley. When I choose to move off, I will push the ground away with a slight sweeping motion. I have estimated the position of my centre of mass and know how far forwards or backwards I can lean before becoming unstable.

Now all I have to do is let myself go.

Woh! And my first thought is that the coefficient of friction of the pavement is so much less than the path I was standing on a second ago and I think 'what kind of thing is that to think?' and then it's like the pavement has turned into an unpredictable version of a running machine and when I hit a little pebble there's that nervous flood you get in your fingertips when you very nearly trip over or slip on a stair and then I'm grabbing his shoulder to steady myself and just laughing, laughing until I see an old lady having this much trouble just walking along but she can't take off her unsteadiness when she's bored of it and she doesn't have anyone left to grab but anyway I'm slightly losing what little nerve I had and I can't stop thinking what if I fall and kiss the pavement so hard that I'll have to turn my unfaithful face back to him with a smile like a ruined pier, spitting blood and teeth into cupped hands?

Dogs of New York

You weren't singled out for attention in any of the guidebooks
I read but you're an attraction in your own right, even for
someone who's scared of the snarlier of your number.
You did get a page in TimeOut that week,
it being Hallowe'en and certain New Yorkers liking to dress up
their pooches for parading purposes (canine *and* human).

That's where the two black terriers in matching witch hats
and capes must've come from. You maintained your dignity,
paws trilling through that fast-forward walk and looking ahead
so you wouldn't have to see your partner in fashion crime.

And then you, you on the subway platform with the grey pin curls
and a shiny nose I've seen on teddy bears,
you stare at me as if to say it's completely normal
for a dog to be toted in a customised sports bag.
The ventilated panel under your tail means you needn't
be buffeted by self-produced hot air, only the
syncopated pre-breeze of the metallic A-train
that gives you a sudden comb-over and quizzical look.

Maybe you know the other dog-in-a-bag I saw, the one
on Staten Island ferry. He was a little rougher round the edges,
mutt to your lavishly named, catalogued lineage,
so maybe not. I could hook you up some time, if you like.

Central Park that day was alive with you.
The frothy white and tan little lady, yes, you, prettytoes,
you think you make the world a better place.
Perhaps you're right to, considering your neat haunches,
eyewear model ocular brightness and the way
you wear your tail like a pedigree pennant.
Your claws are more used to tick-tacking across
genuine hardwood floors, the sound of a concert pianist
waiting for a manicure. Mud is a challenge to you.
You are not surprised when other dogs pull on their leads,
wanting a sniff of your tight little bottom.

It's not like that for you, is it, ugly dog? Resting by a bench,
you're more rotting manatee than dog.
Your blunt jaws would drown an intruder in drool
before you tasted so much as a drop of red.
Your assorted teats speak of one too many litters.
And yet, and yet, your owner holds his breath
to scoop out your food from a tin each morning
and ties it up in scented bags after digestion.
Your faith in your unlikely loveability is steadfast.

The sausage dog is less confident.
You waddle along next to an expensive buggy
bearing cargo that, you suspect, has demoted you.
It's the progeny of a couple whose union was announced
in The New York Times. They used to baby talk you
but these days they're less interested and you catch
mention of keeping doors shut and how dogs are, thankfully,

less likely than cats to smother a baby.
They shouldn't give you ideas like this.
The high yap of a leaf-romping younger version of you
draws a wistful whine from untameable depths.
You remember what it was like to be all feet and ears
and hope, needing nothing more than a romp
and a sniff and a stroke and a bowl of meaty chunks.
But still, someone's always got it harder.

How are you managing, mangy labrador?
The marker-penned cardboard says you've lost
everything except each other. You can barely focus on
the slow-growing pile of coins in the styrofoam cup.
You and your warmth are all he has.
May you never walk past the pre-war apartment block
and look in to see the cosseted white poodle reclining
just to the left of the concierge's desk,
cooling its overfed belly on the marble veneer.
And may anyone who happens to be carrying
a flesh-warm pastrami sandwich on them
open it up, remove one of the ten layers of meat,
and drop it somewhere near your tired snout.

Dogs of New York. There are so many of you that
it's impossible to mention you all but if
you particularly mind that I've missed you out
or can't identify with any of your number listed above,
bounce a bark on your double glazing to say, like,
throw me a bone here, and I'll see what I can do.

CHRISTOPHER HORTON

Woolwich

'I love the noise of men. That is why I love Woolwich. It possesses no external
beauties, no excellences of line or feature, it is tricked with no fair clothing. To love
Woolwich one must love one's kind'
The Outer Circle: Rambles in Remote London, Thomas Burke, 1921

Sit tight in a beat up old van –
belongings jumbled and battered,
A to Z read cover to cover.

Let the cat's eyes guide you
to a new home, yours.
Be drawn to the east.

Keep your hands
in one another's coat pockets
like shy, restless children. Don't worry.

Find Woolwich proper: no line or feature,
no form or function. Unlock the door
of a cold flat above a betting shop.

Find the welcome committee –
a group of youths queuing up
to half-inch your stereo.

Find the thriving local economy –
a line of illegal cab drivers
parked up by the station.

Familiarize yourself
with drizzle. Take in the faint stench
of Beckton Sewage Works.

Enjoy the view – a dodgy dentist surgery
above a card shop, a high-rise
decorated with underwear.

Eat fish 'n' chips off your lap.
Tune the TV. Find no reception.
Collapse on the couch you've just dragged in.

Wake up in the warm backwash of old Kent.
Stuff to unpack. Wake up. Hear the market,
the carefree laughter of men.

Hear the murmurs of a crowd,
the calling and selling,
the local street preacher, whistling.

Wake up. Know you have arrived.

Goldfinger Moves into Balfron Tower

"I want to experience, at first hand, the size of the rooms, the amenities provided, the time it takes to obtain a lift, the amount of wind whirling around the tower and any problems which might arise from my designs so that I can correct them in future." Erno Goldfinger, who lived with his wife Ursula in Balfron Tower for two months from February 1968

What goes, Erno? I'm looking right back at you,
                        out across the graticule of junctions and up,
                        up to where surely you still stand on a pulpit-

balcony, gimlet eyed, dressed in a ushanka
                        and bespoke suit – English cut.
                        The morning light kicks in and in a blink

this becomes the first day of your experiment
                        for elevated living. Flat 130, 26th Floor.
                        Inside, your books vie for shelf space

like siblings, each one outdating the next,
                        their spines wrinkled and flexed
                        years after the rush of a first reading.

Whose treatise on form and function inspires you most, Erno?
                        When Le Corbusier leaves you cold, do you turn
                        to Adolf Loos or dear Walter Gropius?

And tonight, when you pour Russian Champagne
                  into your new neighbours' glasses will you look them
                                in the eyes and promise a new world?

The room behind you lies like an idea,
                  adjusts to its precise proportions, its tailored line.
              The light switches in the doorframes are revolutionary!

How elegantly Ursula walks the corridors, holds the flats
                  of her hands against the newly painted walls,
              takes the scent of each lick as if inhaling magnolia.

Tenancy: 2678AM

Now, Mrs Murphy,
I know it's come as a shock
but you see the flat's not *yours*.
The Association owns it.

Let's just say you had it on extended loan
due to your predicament
and a whole list of *needs*
we assessed in your *Needs*

Assessment. Remember,
when you *needed* us, how you turned to us
with your three children
– each with their own complex *needs* –

and how we gladly placed you.
Look, the repairs
you desire are minor,
an inconvenience for sure, but minor,

and we've got to think of the public purse.
Naturally, there's a list
of people in situations
that are *worse*, far *worse*.

These people I talk of would die

for your level of support.
Believe me, if only you knew
how lucky you are

and we've another unit lined up.
Out of the area, yes; smaller, perhaps,
but suitable, appropriate –
I'd live there myself. We'll even help you

transfer your belongings,
just don't you worry.
We're very accommodating
to tenants that work

with us. Never you mind
what we'll do with it when you move.
We're your landlord, your social landlord.
We look after your interests.

Now tell me, when can I collect the keys?

Rent Man's Note

Yes, I have missed you Ms Maud,
on that monthly round from Pitfield Street

to Hemsworth Street in N1 gloom.
I have even missed your yard's assorted junk:

a punctured chair, shards of mirror glass, a TV stand,
the crooked plastic number 6

mounted lop-sided on your pock-marked door.
You will remember me, Ms Maud,

as a pale and dumb-faced questioner,
a dog-eared sheet of names clinched

to a flimsy clipboard, held in sweaty palms,
and you will know me as the young man

who asked you why you hadn't paid the rent.
Do not think I cared for it, Ms Maud,

the unenviable duty passed on to me
of waiting in the cold for you,

in nylon shirt and mismatched tie,
of giving testimony to the breach of acts and clauses

that never seemed to find full-stops,
or that I prepared the papers *eagerly* for court,

or wanted the judge
to call your name and mine.

Guam

After you left me for what felt like a life time
in the dead heart of winter, its chilling clasp,
for your sister's pre-wedding junket to Guam –

to drink pink cocktails poured by sparkling-eyed
waiters, to lie on white-sand beaches
the length of the High Street, or longer still,

to do the water-sports I would only ever write of,
to swim with laughing dolphins, instructors called Brad,
turtles the size of most domestic satellite dishes –

I walked the streets of South London, eating
pasties and patties from brown paper bags,
spelt out your name with dirty coffee spoons,

slept with your unwashed clothes, the ones you'd left,
aimlessly took buses to while away the hours –
the numbers of which I couldn't now recall if you asked –

passed through Catford, Lewisham, Forest Hill, New Cross,
measuring the distances between each place
by thoughts of you, having fun with Brad in Guam.

WAYNE HOLLOWAY-SMITH

In Defence of Acrimony

What if light slowed to "human" speeds? If it bathed
us in a flux of slow motion images, to the point
of being slower than our own movements? Jean Baudrillard

She must have been there in front of me, but the muffled
I'm sorrys found their place within the club, lost

amongst the bobbing bowl-cuts, Slazenger tracksuit tops
and chorus of Pulp's 'Common People'. I could feel sobs,

the heave of a chest, her arm wrapped around my shoulder.
Yet my ears were blind to the flux of excuses,

my eyes still set on her lounging figure
in my favourite black dress, on the club's leather sofa.

The back of his hair, half of her face – eyes closed –
heads bobbing on each other's surface;

all five fingers of his right hand draped over the white
of her thigh; left hand curving beneath her chest,

her palm balled, flexing slow beneath his royal blue flares.

Coco Lachaille

The back of her hand placates my cheek;
'It's just an act! Are you ok?' Before I reply
she's gone and the hostess announces
'Miss ... Coco ... Lachaille!'

She enters, stage left, charlestons clumsily.
A glut of men watches as she struts,
playful *rubato*, cha-cha kicks, twirls a parasol
like a walking-stick, 'til *oops!* she stumbles,

willingly, throws a candid glance, blows
bubbles with a slim black pipe. I try
to reconcile with last night, but now
her hair is candyfloss pink, folded beneath

a feathered head dress. I stare at her painted face:
white, her blue-rimmed eyes, a single red line
traced on the down of her cheek. I'm fixed
on her lips as she flashes a smile, winks on a beat,

bends to reveal a glimpse of what they came for;
teases the crowd forward in their seats. *Accelerando*:
now the swirls throw up her petticoat's *tulle tiers*;
she spreads the polka-dot parasol, snaps it shut

on the splash of a cymbal. *What applause!*

her velvet corset's disappeared along with the pipe,
replaced by a finger to lips, *broderie anglaise*,
pantaloons. She spins and cocks her foot: *Fin*:

the parasol reopens, she drops into splits.

Beloved, in case you've been wondering

that old man so adamant that he take our picture
on our first date, as we queued outside The Fiddler,
he with his white eyebrows and moustache –
timeless as a clown behind the bulb's flash;

the same one we swore was on stage at Live 8,
craning that big lens our way, between Elton John's legs
and his piano stool, proud as a drunk colonel

and who stuck his head out from a whale's mouth
as we ate 99s on a wooden bench by the Thames,
happy as snowmen:
                                        he's not lost to us; I saw him on the 176,
gaunt and languid – eyes shut – hugging his camera
as he slept. When I read your text, *I'll forgive you…not yet*,

something flashed across his face. I saw his finger flicker.

Dilly Boy

As my friends lean on bars, or recline content
in restaurant seats, I stand alone, burlesque the thirties –
a throw back as I position myself on the Meat Rack,
loiter along the Dilly and in Burlington arcades.

Set apart by the rouge on my cheek, purple sweater
(subtly rolled to the neck), the taper of fur outlining
my gracile figure, a flagrant stance:
twisted hand on fulsome hip.

Still pretty slim, I'd be celebrated on the lips of men
in certain circles, But hated by the powdered, hardened faces
as I'd queer their patch, pout on corners, catch the eye
of every closet queen in town – *ooh vada that bona ecaf* –

hoping for the end of 7/6, for *something special*
round the back, for some wealthy gent
in a handsome suit to take a shine
and I'd be kept
                        a waif-like secret
from the wife, a wanton bit-on-the-side.
Swept from back-street rooms
to the warmth of his second home:

plush carpet, the lampshade's glow
on the gramophone.

Making infrequent visits, he'd seek
to educate my *ignoble* posture,

gradate from calling me *love* and making me
do things *she never could*, to being struck with admiration,
rapaciously lapping at my sense of style.
Changing his wardrobe to mirror mine,

he'd imitate my manner, painting his face in private
the way I publicly display my own,
covet my countenance, and earnestly correct my diction,
sniping at my lack of appetite.

But, when the Gentleman's CLUB
turns its punters to the street, I shrink home
to my lonely flat and know, decadent and wide-eyed
as I am,
            I couldn't have taken it.

Note: The Dilly Boy was an effeminate rent boy, frequently seen in London's West
End in the late 1920s and early 1930s.

Oil

*He spent his final hours greasing and inserting high-scoring Scrabble tiles
into Marie.*

That should be the summary
below my sombre broadsheet box.
My hands and forearms still slippery -
no swarfega concoction could strip them -
I'd skid repeatedly out of the coffin
on the way to the crem. It'd be one, two,
pallbearer demeanour,
three, and damn - he's out again!

(Well pick him up!
Have some dicking respect!)

And Marie, camped in the front pew,
your M&S net barring mosquitoes
and prying eyes, I like to hope
you'd still clutch that pink bottle,
a tear of oil dribbling down the side.

Hypoversion

"...a disorder in which sexual desire is lower than that found in other men and women of the same physique, and which is insufficient to satisfy an average normal healthy sexual partner ... Many men noticed a similar effect during the bombing of London."

The Sexual Perversions and Abnormalities, Clifford Allen

The unseen Blitz,
buttoned into the city's trousers,
as chambers, ports, libraries crumbled
like cake, like felled dragons
bellowing smoke and rage:
silence in the bedrooms.

Those men left –
the wheezy, those not quite eighteen,
just forty-one, those with parents
juggled between countries,
those with vital jobs,
so lucky to have an excuse,
lay supine by sweethearts
as their skyline was pot-shot.

On nights when the sirens' invasion
wasn't too sharp, they might feel
a tap, a brush of breasts against the shoulder,
but the hand, lips, the firm, willing curves

would be gently pushed aside, grumbling
and nursing a hunger
rationing shouldn't touch,
while their partner, healthy but for the flat feet
pinning him to London,
stared at the ceiling: blank

and then suddenly covered
in a paper chase of embargoed photographs:
holes, pits, disappeared shops, jagged black logos,
all those snapped by amateurs then seized by suits
for fear of letting on
that perhaps
the lights might not come on again
all over the world.

Koumiss, or Shark's Fin Soup

For Clifford, the white man's intrigue
in eyeing those outside
the skin group that reddens
and blisters at a sniff of sun
can be likened
to the briny mass of arms
you order on holiday to impress,
or boot-start conversation,
or just to test your tongue, gauging
unexpected pleasure
against the visual wall.

He himself has been imagining
the gradations
and mottled inconsistencies
below the wool A-line
of the hazel maitre d'
at Plenty's. He's been dying
to unbutton and examine
the swarms of smooth Osaka girls
trotting about St Paul's,
placing his pinkish arm
next to their palest lemon.

The tawny French rogue
sticking her tongue out at the driver

of the bus he is on
and she cannot get on
is honey to the gaze, charcoal mane
a thick lick, almost too weighty
for her kisscurl of a body.

And this morning, the urge
to unwrap and unwrap
that satsuma sari, spinning
the naked girl with her clay nipples
out of it like a teak toy,
the inky flourish of her hair
signing off, then coming to rest.

But it is a holiday, belongs in the book
on abnormalities, malversions
which he is drafting.

He buttons up the Osaka girls once more,
scans the bus floor till the French girl
hisses "*merde*" and gives up,
pretends the sari is sackcloth,
the girl inside a chipped dummy.

When the maitre d' returns,
he quips
about her accent
and orders chips.

In the fantasy of screwing your teacher

Neither of you suggests it
explicitly. He asks if you'd like to see
some rare Ashbery he has.

His office is not spotless,
but nor does it hold the carcass
of a Happy Meal box

or a sad, spent scratchcard
or a Coldplay album
or a Newton's Cradle.

Kurosawa discs maybe.
You slide into a kiss, and his arm
does not knock the answering machine,

his ex-wife's voice yawning that while
she's aware there's probably some naïve,
half-dressed undergrad there with him,

Charlotte and Mac need shoes,
his payments are late, and Jack
has been felt up by Akela.

He maintains a poker face
with a whacking great erection.

Good underwear. No brand.

He does not scrabble around, cursing
that he used his last condom
on your classmate.

He does not ask you
to go down on him
but is gently amazed

and reciprocates. And of course
it's ridiculous-good.
He treats your body

like a £10,000 cake,
jokes and rolls you on top
and you - you -

make him lose control.
Though you can't guess
whether he's had two or two hundred

in his time, you know he has never
come this hard. He does not quote Pound
as he moves in and out,

nor does he break down
halfway, sobbing about his job
and repeating your age like a mantra.

As you lie there afterwards,
he tells you something
he's never told anybody.

Either it doesn't end,
or at the door, neither of you
asks what happens now.

ANNIE KATCHINSKA

The acrobat's daughter

ate cream cakes and wrote the word 'beautiful',
unsteadily, in red pen, said *And you have to love yourself*
as she poured the cheap rosé

we choked on and only liked kissing
outside the tent while inside a pyramid of clowns
toppled over to delighted applause, and she bit

my ear, said clowns were mosaics, didn't
elaborate. She never did. She let me tie clusters of gems
round her ankles and throat, pointed to bruises, sore spots

where gymnasts with whirling batons, magicians
wielding saws, painted lips and hands
had all tried. She cracked her knuckles and spoke German,

smudged red around her eyes, said red
was the colour of disintegration, only I noticed she said
the same thing when her eyes were turquoise, purple,
jade, orange or blue. She let me watch her

practising somersaults on Sunday afternoons; let me
hold her but whispered that a woman's body was

a natural deformity, someone had written that, she said;
let me buy her sweets she dropped
in long grass, like unwanted flowers. All colours hurt.

Summer in the City

This afternoon postcards with the Queen's head on them
have been quietly disappearing from the soggy racks, as dozens
of us have scrawled *I MISS YOU IT'S AWFUL* on the back,
not knowing where to send them. Or so I like to think.
Though perhaps there are others whose knees buckle on buses
crashing through Catford, sometimes, when Crazy Bus Lady, a local
celebrity, throws back her head to howl 'Amazing Grace'
at us, the rattling cattle. There must be others who notice
rain-beaten café tables and secluded spots in parks
where someone is missing, who pass through a square
                                    remembering
its Legoland equivalent. By the way, the woman we saw
in her black and white silks and painted misery
is still there, sobbing on the street corner as if all her bones
are breaking to pieces, the hat by her feet glinting toothily
with pound coins. Everywhere I go I hear brass bands.

Healer

You pulled me through scabby streets
into a lift where drawings of fleshy girls
peeled from the walls. I was to be healed.

The apartment of cats breathing dust, cut-outs of kittens
and roses and shining blue eyes was meant to be a kind of heaven.
Black-draped, she gripped my hands and whispered, *Yes, yes.*

Yes, yes as you prodded the craters in my skin, said my face in home
                                                                    videos
hurt you. – I imagined you, piously trembling as I ate lollies, ran
down a beach caked in salt and sand. – There were thousands

of eyes then, and fur against my legs as she slurped
holy water, scratched airy crosses, spat
in my face and moaned at the floor,

you hovering like the cruelest flower.
I tried to speak to you but my mouth was full
of roses, the light was smothered by cats

her fingers lashing at my red marks and blisters
as far off somewhere you pressed yourself
against a wall and yowled at me to pray.

These days I remember the itch on my elbow

as we came home, you sniffing and cooking me bland potatoes,
running me endless baths, making a mental note:

things will always be *wrong*. We send you photos you dislike,
and you sit in your dressing gown skimming
the scraps of alien things, our wonky grins;

we think of your living room full of flawed children,
faces slammed down, chewing dust. How sick we are, you wheeze,
how sick we are.

Super Extra Gravity

kissing skirt unfurls in the alley • tender-stemmed
glassware dangled from tame fingers • a cinematic
gin bar brawl • your surrender to ultra texts • forgotten
green teas cooling in the crush • the silver-brimmed
purse slinks out of sight • melt perfect spheres of ice
• cherry stalks idle in the bowl • every loaded thought
teased out • pale silk wears at the cuff • empty high
heels parade the stairs • twirl the heirloom parasol
• a stack of newspapers concertinas across the rug •
the feeling I'm a pebble beach you just walked across

Seam

The dress, as though made from wax peel imprints
of a thousand fingers, is buxom, even on the hanger.

Worn, its hedgerow-depth textures encase skin
networked with incessant responses: allure blush,

feather itch, lichen slink. It begs for voluptuary touches
along the seam of each curve, kick of spine; limbs

that long for a close palm through satin, silk, cotton,
then calico – voracious for threads to unravel.

Memory Trick

You remember with ease the first four books of the Bible,
13 bars of 'Moonlight Sonata' – but only with eyes shut –
all the words to 'Oklahoma' and 'Empty Saddles on the Old Corral'.

The Illustrated Constellations of the World is a dot-to-dot
of freckles on your arm. A letter device tunes the guitar. Count back
your decades with a legend of knife-slips, dress sizes, deleted

addresses. Transfer lessons learned to the ice tray – to swirl
in the gin glass or store each element, unique in compartments
of a haberdasher's chest. Remember experiments: one burns, one
                                                            sinks,
another implodes. Leave blanks for things you don't yet know.

Luminaire

After Low at the Shepherd's Bush Empire

in the spotlight's vesper glare   I'm stripped
into exposure   my micro details blanked —
          lights   spin open their skirts
till my wax profile   stages a collapse
beneath shade   or I obstruct the dust
caught in the flukes of light   lit like prop
cigarettes twirled through   fat smoke
fingers of space outside the light   as note
against note   moulds   the air's bloom
sinks my skin   my ears thread in
the distinct tones   glide:
          as counterpoint   our lungs shift

Dry Stone Walls

You can find me in the Xs, marking random dates in my teenage
                                        diary.
In the felt-tip dots that mark keys of the piano, one black smudge
                                on the middle d, e, f#, g.

Looking closely at my left ear you'll notice it's been pierced three
                                times, the right ear twice.
My carpet's fluff could provide a clue.

There is something to the perfect hot-rock holes in my oldest jeans,
the certain degree to which I singe my toast.

Or, how my hand remembers the grip of its fountain-pen fist;
my collection of handbags, dresses, hairclips and LPs.

It will help you to see the picture my fingernail traces on your back
while you tell me a story to send me to sleep,

with a boy named Cauldron, who lives on the beach in a cave
carved from diamond, and his best friend Finch, a girl you base on
                                me. Tonight

to catch crabs, Cauldron smashes limpets from the rock pools with his
blunt knife. Finch threads them onto seaweed lines. They wait in the night,
befriending sea birds and fishermen, until Cauldron pulls up the line heavy
with lobster, which they boil on the beach just to see it turn pink

Under cover of your studies, I escape to fields hemmed with dry
stone walls. I climb, giddy, over each wooden stile and tug
        at the heather, the fleece caught on barbed wire.

I have a rucksack packed with a grown-up's sandwich, a pen and
pad to record my observations: there are three cows
        in a neighbouring field, a slight stream on the hill –

it may yet rain. But I'm the only person here, I'm hypnotically
                                        alone.
Wishing me asleep, you're woozy with clues: what to make of my
                                        fanged tooth?

Go, I think. Snag yourself on it.

CHRIS MCCABE

Buttercup

I put a buttercup under my chin & yellow vans go past –
some say RENEW GLASS, others SASH WINDOWS.

USB cables & leads run through my copy of Sophocles –
Oedipus : this is a sign, the pact seals my fate.

After the hospital we brought him back for the first time
– shook up in the harsh responsible ache of love –

we chose him a book to show what he meant to us:
it was too dark to see we were reading *Kidnapped* by RLS,

the lamp burned too bright to read. His escape came when
we went to the sea to see what was hilarious, each wave

crashed its comedy plates between my toes as he was thrown
across my shoulders. At last he knew that two thirds of the world

was what he thought each time he wet himself

George Orwell

I thought the baby was George Orwell & that's why
I treated him so well. There was all ways a sense
of the sado-masochist about this, as I once saw
a sign ALL JAZZ NOW £2 & went to the desk
to insist I paid more. I thought I still had ten minutes
left for the ONE HOUR GALLERY but the artists
were in the back drinking bottles at Polish-strength.
This pushed me mainstream as I started to see the
question-marked shaped tumbleweeds. Whenever I
allow someone to be served before me two things
can happen : a) the wine bottle runs dry & I wait
for the decorking of another or b) the barman forgets
my philanthopy and serves all new-comers. By the
time the ATM device says CONSENT it feels like
an arranged-marriage. God kills kittens when you
think bad thoughts but sometimes it's hopeless :
she comes in topless from the grass with a grip on
some shears, above her the Vs of swifts that never
come-down. I said to her : the oggyoggyoggy is the
last refuse of the untalented, she replied : your sense
of humour is so dark you have your own apartheid.
The boy had just graduated from the University of
Snail (no career fast-track but at least you would own
your own home). Hours later, the boy asleep,
we walked together the emblazoned
afternoon, through the showroom of tombstones.

Night Ward

When the boy was incarcerated he became
convinced that a laptop-broker would steal
his last labelled biscuit from the communal
kitchen. He thought the much-discussed
panopticon was a poor wafer replacement.
He stared-out the red LCD lights on the machine,
hand-processed shots of dolphins' eyes. Incey-
wincey shadows like 70s moths. Garish brocades
of paisley. Doctors in bowties appeared – neck
presents for patient vampyres. Jenga-bricks like freights
from A-road towns, decrowned. The boy wants
to bring the Night Ward back to life as if all
previous patients failed, by choosing to leave
behind a small piece of their own silence

Red

Ten words for how she is : she said sorry for my pain as she gave
birth.
Her brother was smitten with the child – & though no freak –
fingers coiled foil umbilicals.

On starry nights in December the jukebox was tendentious.
With the afterbirth arrived the text : *no more drinking for you* –
four weeks later the pram rolled on its own down the tube,
she took the can the drunk commuters offered her, alighted,
pointed towards Canary Wharf – which she hated – & said
"I fucking love this City".

She got off on Red the way I had on amphetamines,
I got off on The Word the way she did on Red.

Words for her brother : take the Northbound Northwards & don't
fail.

Red for her was what some hear in a name (names came in colours),
Red communist stars on the tree, so Christ was at rest.
She said Castro's brother was hardly Young Flesh, at the time
she was wearing a red T-shirt : UNWRAP ME FOR CHRISTMAS.
Talked of other red things : migrating to Wandsworth on the
Central Line, a career as a socialist.
On Pay Days we went to the dogs & put it all on Trap 1
(the boy adrift in the boat of honey sailed away on a sea of sleep).

Trap 1 won. And Yes, she did look a little like the woman
in Picasso's *Pierreuse, la main sur l'epaule.*

She accepted the can. The pram rolled down the tube.
She stood up in dark music & danced in red silks.
She carefully fed the child & poured more shiraz.
A vulva of red lipstick around the neck of the glass

a baby bottlenecked in a celluloid pool
emerged a clay doll – he breathes! –
& stunned us to the wall. His birthmark
– new borders – embossed in red on his neck.

The Rules of Attraction

The rules of attraction are : it's
happening. The rules of attraction
are : red. The rules of attraction
are : time cuts a hand. The rules of
attraction are : common ground is
sliding. The rules of attraction are :
counterfeit. The rules of attraction
are : conception. The rules of att
raction are : amendments of your
self for someone who doesn't know
you. The rules of attraction are :
adrenalin pours sodium glutamate.
The rules of attraction are : honestly.
The rules of attraction are : reddish.
The rules of attraction are : miscon
ception. The rules of attraction are
: amend -----------

The one rule of attraction is that it has already happened.
The one rule of attraction is deception.
The one rule of attraction is time cuts.
The one rule of attraction is already ash.
The one rule of attraction is rules.
The one rule of attraction is no rules.
The one rule of attraction is your pulse macaranes at the Reichstag.
The one rule of attraction is it will never happen.

You lifted your neck back to ask, the dog-collar's metal studs did a FIND&REPLACE on the stars. The interpreter once reached out & touched me in the white stasis of the Underground – I had no reason to hear after that. Wolfwhistled at plasticine for years. The tale began of a hackney cab & a Princess, the orange lights went back on & the white pills made tears in the cubicle. It was like we had jumped the queue on falling in. Leave. Stay for one more.

The rules of attraction are : it's already happened.

MARIANNE MUNK

from Lines upon seeing an old, sick man scorned at a public rite

16 / 05 / 08 (for SLW)

O temp
type for Jafar and Schmitt
be thyself the needful documents ·
till London's tall lamps
and her plain trees
are felled with puke
inhale birds' healing gas ·
I have something to send by you
stay a little · O temp
bollards come up cob

12 / 05 / 08

a boot touched a being,
Toby voted boris · Σόλων
well considers it
to be "will obey orders"
its accidents
were in shadow
and its essence
aligned with the window
lit high in the hill basilica · let's trust
substituted idiots under us

18 / 10 / 08

go on, please • flower
vane-drawn •
warm among maples
puking his bearings •
& prim I'll turn pancakes
with my gurn • will
belabour flecks
of heel quorn
& skins of wands
in her unlit wok,
your dead one •

Reminder 37

Collect as much Cultural Revolutionary memorabilia as you can... the market is better than Islington real estate. That sounds like the kind of thing someone writes when they know exactly what's inside, but I don't. Who are you? Care to fill me in? Chinese sign language for Chairman Mao is a straight finger pointing to the left hand side of the chin. Old Revolutionaries will appreciate this. These guys are PROFESSIONALS. Richard Rorty giggles 'she she.' Three boisterous Ghanaian women spontaneously and quite without grounds were on the verge of finishing recording an EP. No guitar, piano, programming or note taking; left-handed wiping, washing, brushing of teeth and masturbation – yes I got my license finally, it took me three years. And whilst the newsletter I spent three weeks writing has changed the world because it was read by the head of the Global Policy Forum whilst they were finishing a paper recommending sanctions reform on Iraq which was released today along with a statement by it and nine other organisations, my mum fell asleep three times while I was waiting (in gown & translucent pants). I only managed to eat a little before I had to get rid of the taste with a raspberry and blackberry petit filous (known in our house as 'pity for you' because they mean you aren't getting a real pudding and thus annoys Mummy, particularly when you add "and I suppose THERE'S bananas ISN'T there?"). I just read the news about the crazy bombings in London. So I hope that you are alive and well and that none of your loved ones are hurt. Maybe you'd like to come visit me in America? Stuff like that doesn't happen here.

A Short Lecture on Marianne Morris

a compleinte. *buxom*, c.1175 – "humble, obedient," suckling bursar.
this shits on O'Hara. cursive sub-prime pervert ogles merkinlike
market for velcro curvature, i.e. *pussy cat sticks! pussy cat sticks!* in
the first one.

it gets worse further on though: log-tying, as if reversible. puts
the "care" back in "careless." her gross boss walks in on her
seamstressing her timesheet into a sorta skirt. these poems beat
poetry on the hardest setting.

rakish shimmer of merbowels every time something's described as
purple. in that respect like Foster-Wallace meets Lorca . . . on acid!
fluorosulfuric acid easing their necks into their throats – poems are
unimportant, it follows that these are not those. Lorca burps purple
(rakish shimmer of merbowels) hemo-mud gurgles. CASSETTE
TAPE IN ANONYMOUS ENVELOPE takes its coffee young,
gifted and black. and its Thames, bongwater – flashflooding in the
background of a lowrider open top bus.

Marianne Morris!
lost in a forest,
with her skin so porous
and her blood so ferrous!
not afraid
of the woodland chorus,
the geckos bright,

and the moles omnivorous!
fierce as a
tyrannasaurus!
Marianne! Marianne!
Marianne Morris!

there's this bit where its protagonist, HARMONY, breaks his chin
off to show everybody that's where E-Bay is. it's like that – she
should have got a woman to write some of them. in another, anyone
with a beard is taking a nap. so it's kind of vivid in that way.
"irresistible" but with a funny voice – like maybe "ireezeeestable,
homes!" like over-the-top spectacle-latino. the reader starts to feel
this OK:

pinking shears
tin snips
pruning shears
secateurs
loppers
throatless shears
poultry shears
trauma shears
jaws of life
about, you understand, a pinprick of cash – what that can do. then,
if you really want to know, there are these patches of Medusa ethics
gristle. the vividness and the warmth drains away. these segments
have been invited to waste reluctance on jurisprudence, and they
have refrained. hem stuff. long ago. their words look like Middle
English words that happen to have the same spelling. they aren't

fucking verdant so don't pretend like they are. they aren't even
ivied o"r. this town is a Big Top-shaped crater too.

and then phew! it's OK and the MET are shampooing a bird or
whatever and the reader's heart like a weary newt resting in wires
borrows the bandage from around brer salmon's throat and his
commercialisation is written on the inside of what the reader
now thinks is his bracelet (fool!) or slinky and there's the thing
about either rescuing or going jogging and Allah has this confetti
collection that is all eyes perforated from Scooby Doo "surveil &
persecute"-portraiture and the reader – the reader has messed up.
he's scheduled his wedding on the same day as his birthday. what's
he going to do.

She Stroy

(He nodded and she knew she was allowed on the bus)

He nodded and she knew she   he
Noddded and she knew she was
He knodded and she new
she was allowed on the bus
and she knew she was

She knew shenew
he nodded and she knew she was allowed on the bus
Nod nod and she new she was
A loud on
Dead and new she
Allowed on the bus
No ded and she
Knod dead and she knew
she was
A low on a bus
he know   dad cough
he's now dead and she

all wet on the bus
a low wedding the bus
he's not ded and she's allowed
on the bus
Where can we eat in the bus
Is this a hub

                    is this a hub/where can I piss in
the bus
And then she knew   Somewhere to eat?
          He nodded on   and onto a a body

Somewhere for sex on the bus?
          crawling over bodies   around the rules of the bus
                            Madame he is
partly he he he!
He nodded and she's bust
This is like a film
And she knew she was

                    she's sewn in
to The bus
to The double upper   she's sewn in

                    The seen on the bus
with the non-dead
She's in the scene
He nodded.

In ninety minutes the shot

(where is she?)

ends
steps off/onto the bus she knew

he nods

she knows

is this the

café? are you madame
He enacted a nodding

She impassioned a thinking

Rattle heads against the bus

nod nod

hallowed the hotel

Is this the way madame?

In nine miles the scene (where is she?)
shot dead the scene beginning again

with coloured filters with

She
He nodded du-duh du-duh du-duh du-duh
she 's allowed to move on
This time

with extra filters

de da Mister
is this the sex madame?
she she knew she
de dah de dah

The Horsey Mail

I send this to you by overnight horse.
He whips east like the 277.
In Highbury I stare at my ceiling
and see you yesterday, from the top deck of a bus,
cycle down Kingsland Road.
You wobbled a bit past Dalston Junction
(was it the wind or the traffic or me?),
with your legs – I thought I saw –
shaved for aerodynamics. And anyway,
everything and nothing rides on him,
and the road surfaces are uneven
and his forelocks are wavy
and so is your hair when it's longer
and that makes me lonely,
so give him oats and blackcurrant jam,
James, and damn the vitamin tablet
in my throat that keeps me awake;
it's not the morning without you.
And forgive him –
he may have nothing to give when he gets there.

Dependency on Oats

Call me the handmaiden of porridge –
it impels me to stir then shapes itself, fills me with greedy rapture.
April's *Art Monthly* hangs over the clothing rack in the bathroom.
My purpose is in the saucepan on a gas ring in the kitchen.

It is not solid though it is consistent.
If it gets hot, it thickens; if it goes cold, it thickens.
In my ratio of milk to water to brown sugar I am steadfast.
I scrape and tap my spoon as if one gesture leads to another.

Today I will assume untold guises without awareness –
pedestrian, daughter, acquaintance, passerby, redhead –
but porridge is porridge. Liquid and heat have brought me to this
repeated figure-of-eight and it is habit – breakfast.

Winter Evening with Nuts

It's not quite rain, that's just how London sounds
when the clocks have gone back.
In the sitting room I eat from a jar with my fingertip.

If only I could taste the unsalted peanut butter.
If only I could read the Penguin Rhyming Dictionary in bed
to a lover. 'Elbow', I'd declare, turn to entry 12 –

'oboe, hobo, flambeau, mambo, combo, rainbow,
poncho, rondo, rouleau, tableau, pueblo,
memo, Sumo, lino, rhino… Should I stop?'

'No.'
'capo, chapeau, hippo, typo, tempo, Velcro,
metro, retro, Rousseau, trousseau. Also – fatso, scherzo,

ditto, Shinto, tiptoe, gusto, yo-yo, Tokyo.'
'Bravo.'
My vocabulary would manifest something undeniable.

Instead it's 6.24 pm, and it was dark two hours ago.
So many nuts in one jar, and this is what they come to –
closed curtains, the extravagance of imagination, the sofa.

On Unpredictable Weather Conditions

Once, in Ohio, I faced a tornado.
The sky was a dirty curtain, and then rainfall –
a bit like tonight in East London on your futon
with the weather at the window and you asleep to my left,
only there I was alone and calmer.

This pillowcase, left by your ex, has a nice pattern.
I wish it didn't. Perhaps she had significance
and a fabulous lilac jacket. I want to stay longer
under your winter duvet. One day
I'd like to put your paper clips in order.

See how I take the side furthest from the door?
In the wind in the night in a booming Columbus suburb
in the eye of meaningless panic most of life ran for cover.
But here, mad with trepidation, I run towards your cyclone.

anti-gravity belt projects,
or each man for himself & god against them all

a derelict hotel is not a tree . with its diverging
lines a tree is thin like the compulsion to make
tidy, to avoid all contact with speculative fiction,
while (in its place) a derelict hotel is thick with
overlap

layer'd structures often have (unmarry'd) men
visiting relatives frequently plus giant robots of
simon bolivar on robot horses triumphant . at a
certain height thoughts of simone weil in just
dungarees & the honest man's revenge derive
coherence from the total absence of a roof

neither wholly contain'd nor disjoint (from
hallow'd satellites) relations are seen at a
distance, no obstacle to knowledge when up-close
both share the same name & given name . the
second is what's known as the blame artist, his
steering oar set too quick to the smoke . the older

has great hair & a word file recording all wrongs an aversion to cooking fat belongs also to this semi-lattice as does the way that lot use dress as a means of thinking about empires in the stars . the communion of saints & pseudo-martyrs has only one possible hall of meeting (the present moment) a derelict hotel whose remaining original colour'd panes are, of course, the origins of grace

her splitting headache & slit eye-ball conjoin with railway tavern facade in the editing (bricolage as morphological innovation) a multiplicity of aspect providing unmarry'd men with access to young cousins at play . by blue light heaven's administratum in their cups & local rough trade on shakiest foundations they comb their bleach'd fringes forward

even with your top button done up sublime it's obvious the floors & ceilings need replacing . above the sixth-floor, traditional forms of contact with the ground (such as appropriateness & the greeks) are valued much less . in a proper system or lunar excursus, the mere lapse of time any given saint or pseudo-martyr travels to reach this particular derelict hotel is ultimately immaterial

as a kid, i went once with my dad to a barber's shop in harringay . we took turns getting our hair cut . remember tho, her question was on naming not social-networks & a red-stripey pole (past or future) is a no longer valid object cries the moon . all the brigands have dismember'd all the ears of all the chic travellers after all, croon the holy fools & gonzo ecclesiasts of chris' cash & carry

rocket-man of valves & mnemotechnologies (flower of south america) like hermes psychopomp gravitating to each lunatic pamphleteer in crush'd luncheonette of our lady by dismal spume, or just to go by rush-light for nerdy girls demure & romping . think speciously on the cramp'd repeats of the décor, on the deconnect'd spaces the younger one who gave to cat-aids religiously will one day get up with speaker-wire

the derelict hotel is a precarious calculation, not a tree but a reticular weave design'd to convoke hagio-variants for genuflexion . re-convening, take pictures of each prayerful life with your eye only & its unblinking blue bulb tracing machine corpses for separate internment . in the lobby debris, wherever young people dress & behave as young people always dress & behave, a moon (polite catastrophe of beauty) scaring saint simone who is there also, shot at without discrimination

Beat London

Not quite raining, not that cold, not late.
I know where to go, and settle to the time,
the pace, the dark. I have the rhythm right.

Wine has hollowed me out like water over stone.
It found some fault and deepened it, till you
could sink your thumb there, pull out a peaty silt.

To St Paul's up Ludgate Hill I carry space as tribute.
It presses out. A couple flag down a beetling cab
and he can't take his hand from the small of her back.

I cross the river, beat my ring against the rail,
slow syncopations to slip myself away from myself
till I'm on dry land. Someone laughs; someone starts to sing.

By Tower Bridge, as I stop to smoke and flick the stub out
into the river, this final theme lifts, pulls something loose,
sends it tumbling in my blood, snagging under muscle,

leaving a root exposed, tender as grazed knuckles, an anemone
in the tide, while the lost matter twitches a little where it lies,
waiting to be reabsorbed, change the colour of my skin.

The streets are almost empty now. Below high-price
living rooms lit flat screen blue I will make my way,
sling my headphones on, choose my drug, press play.

The Statues of Buckingham Palace

One day, old lion, we will stir ourselves,
shake off the bronze and be flesh.

The sash across my breast is blue I think, my hair
the dirty blonde of your pelt.

First we will look over our shoulders - I'll smile
shyly at the young men who've lounged a century

by the pool, then, without comment, you'll
roll your great shoulders and pad down onto the Mall.

I keep my hand warm in the rough tangle
of your mane. We walk past straight-backed generals

dusting the last of the black paint from their coats, while
the gentlemen of state adjust their breeches and steel

swords, clear their throats, and scramble down to the grass.
Along the Embankment we're joined by a few nervous
poets and the occasional nurse. The light is flat, Apollos
blink their olive eyes and begin to tune their lyres;

the muses and graces group with soft calls
to touch each other's pale new skins

with their fingertips. Mythical beasts lope beside us
and the Thames is full of mermaids in pearled scales.

We turn up towards Trafalgar Square, joined
 by a Jesus or two, who have clambered

down from the fronts of churches. A little bemused, they rub
their palms and shiver. The military gentlemen give them
                                                overcoats,

clucking under their waxed moustaches. The Jesuses bob
their heads in thanks, feel in the pockets for tobacco.

Then everyone goes still to watch as you and I, old lion, climb the
                                                steps
to the Gallery and whisper steeply at the key hole, waking the
                                                pictures.

Studio / Arthouse

You wanted to end us then and there,
where we had hidden from the rain
in Hyde Park; pressed in behind me,
your palm on my hip, you buried
your mouth in my neck and said:
'Roll Credits'
          as if you could, as if the thing
were done, as if you'd cut us out to black,
behind the marching band, the punch
of a rock track, as the trees exploded
in the heat, the wet, the right of it.

But we lived. The world is all accident.

                       Now
when I come to meet you with my high heels
tapping on the tiled floor of a Borough bar,
you hold out your hand and ask me for my news.
I can give you days of it, sweetheart,
weeks, when once you were every moment,
each beat began and ended with your name.
I am unspooled, over-exposed, open-ended,
jump-cut and abstract.
                 Let them roll now then
over you, sorry and afraid, as the tide sucks
down the Thames and carries all our time with it.

Spilling Out

What's the half-life of a bright idea?

How deep must it be buried to prevent it
radiating, like trying to stop a bulb's insistent light

from spilling out between fingers, or leavening
the enforced blindness of closed eyelids?

Imagine balancing that hot bulb
on your tongue, with all its brilliant shining.

Now, try closing your mouth.

The Difficulty and the Beauty

The devil / threads his needle, / and the string's a river / fat with fish / that wanted other words for it.

Ars Poetica, Ashley Capps

Sometimes, it's like fishing, perched
on the bank of a body of water
that ripples out to an indifferent horizon.

There's a part of you casting a line
that disappears beneath the water's surly face,
and waiting. Always the business

of waiting– no guaranteed reward beyond
the hook in your gut that pulls you back
to this same place, time and again;

whatever whispers in your ear to cast out
longer, deeper still, in spite of all the junk
that you return: the coke cans, boots and small fries

blindly snagged and hauled into unforgiving light.
There are days on which you wonder
what this so-called work is worth,

this clean-handed trawling of depths,
this wealth of time spent, marked

by the furl and slap of each collapsing wave

like the turning of the next blank page.
Sometimes, it's an empty bucket
or the simple currency of a sunset, brazen

as the sugars in autumn leaves. Sometimes
it's the distant light of stars and peopled windows
that your eyes expand to hold. And sometimes,

it's the next real tug on the line,
the day's catch reeling in.

How to be Black

There's a little of you in everything,
and always someone trying to muscle in
on the act, trying to be the new you.

Mostly, you're cool about it, but
all the attention gets tired real quick–
eyes peering in, eager to strip you back,
layer by layer, until there's nothing left.

Deep down, there's a lot of people scared
that there's more of you around than they
can swallow. By the same token

there's always someone trying to ape you
like a bad fax. *Go 'head*, you say,
*shine as hard as you like. See if I don't
ball my cheeks n' blow your light bulb out.*

That ol' shadow gig's just a day job.
Mostly, you work nights.

Conviction

You're a little too stoned to be doing this, but
Bless you, you're trying. I look past your face
at the ceiling. Bob Dylan and Alice Glass
and glow-in-the-dark stars compete for attention.
Just a man, but still all boy. The Toy Story duvet
Slips down your back and I grip your shoulders
Convincingly.

In the grey of the anti-climax, I ache for what comes
Next and what came before. The scramble upstairs as
I took you by the hand. Dot-to-dot on your freckles
As I wait for breakfast - stale pizza and tea.
I don't love you now
But I did
And I will.

It hurts a little; I wince and refocus on you,
You think that this is a good thing: this means
I like it. I can tell. I read the flicker of triumph
on your Scrunched-Up-Origami-Concentration-Face.

This intensity is unattractive to me.
I want the poised perfection of the prelude; the pout,
The eyelash flutter. The prettiness of the promise.

I don't say any of this. I breathe heavily and pretend to
sleep, knowing that I played my part with precision
If not heart. Conviction is for another night.
Bless you, you tried. I look past your face and at the wall.
All things considered, you did well. I know you were
Only in the mood for a hand-job while you nodded off.

99 Flakes and The End of Something

Puddles of taffeta, weeping ice cream and
Melting eyeliner cried from my aviators;
I was rendered far too dramatic a figure for my liking.
Yesterday, our kisses scribbled plans for forest raves
And decadent fields, mapped contour lines
With bare hands. Only the highlands and rolling meadows.
Valleys and floodplains would have just been a bit slaggy.

A wink of sleep later
and I'm on the heath,
playing out the death
of a romance that lasted
as long as a reel of celluloid.

Office workers had shed their costumes, luxuriating
In the debris of shirts and ties and sunshine and us.
They stared as my rage played up to itself and almost
Made you cry. We acted our parts beautifully; gasps
Gossiped across the cityscape as I flung my bag
Over the grass and my jacket to the floor. An old lady
Forgot herself and started clapping as I stormed off,
Leaving a small trail of stylish destruction in my wake.

If it had been a film, that's when the strings would come in,
I wouldn't have had to go back to get my stuff and make my
Precarious way home.

Or else I would have stacked in my stilettos,
We'd have laughed and made up.
I'd have said
Something profound, rather than cursing that you couldn't
Just chuck me by text like normal people.
I ached for my mum and chocolate, to do away with spectators,
A squishy sofa, pyjamas. Flat shoes.

Every kiss since feels like punctuation
On pages of empty script. Xs mark spots
Where you're not and nothing feels quite as fabulous
As that time I bitch-slapped you on Hampstead Heath.

Such a lot of world

The result rolls in and I watch them celebrate in Chicago
On late night CNN. The television's blue light
Burns cold twilight in my living room, and the tap on my
Window never comes. This would have been our time for
heroes, dancing like the victory's ours.
If he loses, we'll tiptoe through world war three,
Out the city's backdoor and be tearaways for the day.

I bake a lonely apple pie to feel part of something, and
Can't say I feel so forlorn when cutting out pastry in star shapes.
I'll elope with myself across the seas to sing your songs
In a new colour. The representatives will ask me
"Darlin', won't you show us what you look like without skin?"
And the softness which you loved so much will be gone,
Gone as far as the greyhound will take me.

The Detroit bars will welcome me 'cause I bake
Like a true patriot, and I dress the part. Obama will come out
Twisting like a Tarantino film. I'll be real, no longer
Soluble in kohl tears, with your words to keep me company
Between motel sheets when the Motown LP sleeps.
London for now though. I live in it like the ache in my chest,
Like the eyes in my head and the kiss behind my lips.

Dr. Bakunetsu

His name is Japanese for 'explosive heat' –
it's also, he says, unfastening his suitcase's
brass clasps, the name he gives the ailment, taps
the carat of my ribs – "In here, chief?

Right-o, that's a nasty one. No, don't speak.
These things can go off any time, sunshine,
I've seen ones that could atomise Parliament,
your heart's the barrel and this thing, chief,

this is the burning taper. S'only got to leap
like a flea, or a jumping bean, sunbeam,
skip like a record and your whole torso'll
go up like a sack of fireworks. Keep still, chief."

His cigarette tipped with a ziggurat, his teeth
cusped with blood, he makes an incision.
My chest's the seat of something unstable
as the Second Triumvirate, making sleep

impossible. Hot-black as torched heath,
lodged like grapeshot. I've heard such things
are regarded by some as blessings, weapons
to be broken in, stars to leash.

but where do you start? "Hold still, chief!
Almost got the bounder." Steam whistles
from the crack, a stutter of sparks ricochet
off his goggles. He grins. "Wasn't all that deep,

son. Not surprising – you ain't got much meat
on yer." He jauntily applies a sticking plaster.

The Warlock Hits Town

"Biting my truant pen, beating myself for spite,
 'Fool' said my Muse to me, 'look in thy heart and write.'"
Astrophel and Stella, Philip Sidney (attrib.)

He tries it on with a girl from the office:
"I don't tell many people this. I'm actually
quite the ventriloquist. Not the nightclub variety
with the split personality –
one of the originals – old school, baby.

Call me 'The Ringmaster'." Microscale winds
strung to his bandaged fingers, he does the trick,
not 'throwing' his voice, but placing it,
as onto a beermat, on a sudden squall
which ferries it down the girl's blouse,
so her breasts seem to say,
"Hey, it's cramped down here."
"Yeah, let us out."

"I've been training the wind for years," he drawls.
"Not only can I close windows from my armchair –"
he demonstrates with a flourish
"– but I can also do this."
And the croaking hinges of the pub's oak door
whistle the theme from *A Fistful of Dollars*.

A bloke mutters "Wanker" under his breath,
and our hero has it out from under him
like a tablecloth, leaving the crockery of his teeth
only lightly jarred.

'Wanker' resounds in everyone's ears
and a dozen chairs are scraped, heads pivoted
to pinpoint the outburst's source.
The bloke becomes incarnadined.

Later, more success: "So what's it like?"
says this hoyden in a drop-waist. "Knowing the wind."
"She's a shape-changing octopus," he slurs,
"tapping directly into my thoughts,
one of her suction cups latched to me
like a stethoscope. Know what I mean?"

But she coasts away when a name enrages him:
"Njörðr? Don't talk to me about Njörðr.
Njörðr my arse. Where is he? I'll bottle him."

Some clock his moonish complexion,
the dark calligraphy of his features,
his aristocratic wrists
and whisper, "Vampire."

Netting the word,
he disagrees – "Dragon!" – and jokes
that the yards of bubblewrap caught in branches

alongside the A306
are his sloughed skin.

He loses his wallet somewhere in Soho,
frisks stranger after stranger, slavishly,
makes scarves into swinging cobras
as he and his octopus agent stalk through clothes,
industrious as beaters,
sending train tickets, receipts shooting up
like ash.

Getting home, he pukes near a bus shelter
and cuts all his hair off with a knife of wind.

Catullus: Searching for Planet Prince

I. The search continues!

Still skulking out of sight, eh?
Still evading my panoply of scanners,
you who I've scoured the colonies of Mars for,
combing every last spaceport from New Heathrow
to the one they named after great Gordon himself.
Old fashioned as I am, I even raked Shoreditch,
approached anime-eyed pleasure gynoids –
"Give him up!" I snarled, shaking them by the shoulders.
"Tell me where he is, you clock-hearted trollops!"
"Zzt. Between my breasts?" one fizzed. "Between
my breasts? B-breasts, boy? Be –"

Rooting you out's as much of a challenge
as ever faced by Commander Keen, o' pal o' mine.
Come out and face me! Or let's make a date?
Send me a signal from the giant holoscreens.
Why not? Are you holed up
with a bevy of moon-white space vixens, Prince?
You know what they say: "No sweet talk,
no sweet love" – Venus loves a filthy mouth,
a loose-tongued braggadeer.

...

Fine then. Keep shtum.
But save me some of that!

II. No end in sight.

... not if I were Bucky, Captain Bucky O'Hare,
not if I were Adam Strange, John Carter, Buck Rogers,
not if I were fledgling captain Derek Wildstar
with Nova's tongue on the edge of my ear,
nor Gil the Arm, nor Trent Hawkins fleeing Tyrian,
faster than the *Yamato*, faster than Astroboy –
I'd still be down to my last tank of oxygen,
knackered to near stasis-lock
from hunting down this blasted Prince.

Torn Page from a Chapter on Ray Guns

AM Low's 1937 *Adrift in the Stratosphere*, attacked by radium rays from
Mars develop symptoms which force them outdoors. Luckily, their ship's
instruction manual describes how to switch on the anti-radium ray. EE
operas are full of garish and irresistible rays bouncing off force scree
grandiose ray-gun is the sunbeam (this was the era of vacuum-tube
the entire output of the Sun on an invasion force.
WE Johns of Biggles fame gave us *Death Rays of Ardilla* (195
weapons are a conveniently slow-moving form of radiation which
flooring your ship's accelerator. In Arthur C Clarke's *Earthlight*
weapon becomes a stream of white-hot molten iron that punches
spaceships. In Colin Kapp's *Transfinite Man*, 'sodium lamps
penetrate your skin and catch fire. Sunblock is no help.

      In Robert A. Heinlein's *Sixth Column* the horrible 'Pan
USA, which fights back with ray technology that can tune
invaders instantly, their proteins coagulating like a boiled
stun guns have been a standard science fiction prop since
fall over unconvincingly") was a latecomer. Other
nervous system, like Asimov's neuronic whip,
"Berserker" killing machines, implacable
But the death ray in *Silence is Dead*
new electro-gravitic and magneto-

      In Stephen Baxter's *Xee*
starbreaker is a modest hand
destabilise stars. Its red out
gravity waves. *The Zen*
detonating suns. Tho

smoke spouting
blue flames
moving
Luck

BARNABY TIDMAN

Nineteenth Manner

after Richard Burton

Mortlake
shadow of heaven

pierce of machine vision

wristwatch
climbing flesh

Alphabet grip
Al-Jebra
disembodiment at mapping

(seeing one's self)

Low Illumination Side
(orange coloured scale): zero method
'Firstly, the loss of generative power'
centrally-weighted averaging

system.

spout repetition
Twenty-First Manner- Rekeud el air (the race of the member)

quiver of gears, speed of the head
melts language
esoteric tilt
sex drive weighed toward origin

Armistice Day

to lengthen mortlake high street

(grained red) dust lords with aerial room

left in the field-skull push sight

away from place in time

the Barnes actors (lactors) amounting image, booze out lisps
to stall creation and gather thespo
singularity to ending pubs, curved minds

with stiff fingers drawing rain from stores, the moth lords

charge the roots of the eye, absorbing brace of time

an evolutionary impension

crackling fabric of war

limbo rigid
(the lords of ancients would not watch but urge)
the dead river lowers its puss, flashmen of epo-crunch
suit through primal drips (~~sliding~~slide against ~~solid~~drooping air)
whilst barren LActors
can provide stillness, scanned ghost

but to stretch form, to wrap
the colour to termination of your
questions, invasion of content

describe war,
to see the eruption of urges

historic swarm, thought destruction

Spread and Division (Basic Perinatal Matrices)

I

Shadowliths of winter machines
brush the street,
centreless dimensions
filling

52inch plasma in the boot
of the white-van running blank metres
bends suspicion
from sun rays, orbital contemplators, African accents inside that
notch traffic
unknow the will of their machinery, universes of theft-

satellites bite the Thames behind the street-saliva
Pheisar landing on top of a postcode, body hardening with shiver
flexing speed rejects an exterior depth
of mangled instincts
rearing thought backwards,
Pheisar who spells cities lowers his head
accepting just girly 2step
grain

Isis, striking horizonal
whose tiny spine is a hallucinatory median
blazed between the algorithm of animal bones

pied in the water,

Pheisar, climbing gas of lightbulbs
muscling blank space, the fleshing beep of eternity
denting his head with building merchants
tones up the rotting steppes of London
boiling with immigrated hordes
battled around French phonics, Russian digits
sleep machines, zone-dead happenings-

the Van, ripping its breath
sucking in the snares of reflected light
floats at speed between the altered technology,
the land ships, the Africans inhaling acceleration bursts.
Radar shadows bouncing friction tide. Quantums of intention
swarming down the phone hole.

.....

Jeans on a bathroom floor.
leather.
clouds,
streamers, engines,
flesh on water.
sunset.
oil on the tyres,
mirror on the car,
flesh on the mirror.
M.O.T. shacks (toothpaste temperature) unfold flat tunnels,

dual-carriaged tongues licking weather.
Isis pumping light-freeze,
swarming monoliths
=

P-Tsar walked absorbing rebellion
repelling absorption from sky corners.
His eyes swallowed.
Aimed through swarming Russian furs, anarcho dollars
comes the thud of/reverence/insanity of the shock.
his mind fathomed a mile-long, downward echo
survived like an ant
infinitude of re-cognition;

arabesque of ego rotating,
harmonic drive sprawling through a second.
the corner of sky staining. lobes bleeding with shadows.
gauges of the present affected with nations
of time ascend to Babel density-
the thought of weather
lolling from skull-planets,
no extensions to keep shape, repel
absorption.
Eye-beams swung by creeping minds
bordering on mergers,
gold escalators
EC1
sky high statues, aching currency
self-beheading leadership, nation-stone pandering sleep

to Battersea
pain of romanticism
trauma of time, relentless
ecstasy of location
separating psychordinates,
post orgasm of isolation hustling for laughter
(grasping street-hands, remembered direction)
drop-ship mandalas hung from the seventh atmospheric layer
cloud-dust onto insane acres of imagination.
Fray-Seer hustling the laughter of phantoms, warming to the daze
of Malcolm X's echo-less morphine trip,
tears in the far corner of the eighth layer
hang from streaming ice eras---

--- awake in a rash of street clothes
chasing the breadth, brushing oily rain from his logo

behind the mirror (shaving winter)
stubble flashing from the face-paw
eyes calligraphise   worn ice systems
twisted ghosts/ systematic dream

II

NIL 478
NIL 231
NIL 194
a mass of sleek funeral glass
gears through the sooty light of gyratory
bridges, Bermondsey soil
fluttering into the bursting history
of the sun. Registration codes rising, chasing consciousness.
Decay picked up on the migrating language, distributed
as points of light. Bloodless fractures
filling with sun-form. Death reverberating
through unconscious continent

Isis steams with memory
leans towards the ocean, the thump
of healing water. Pheisar boils in high winter
digital glory of un-made buildings. Uncreases silence
in roving high tower. To the sound of porcelain ripping
drops his eyes through storeys,
mouths information
as the cracked lightning
fists and breeds

Διόνυσος

Girl with ridiculous earrings   why do you bother
to slap the boy   we all assume is your boyfriend
and is lolling over   that bus seat   shouting

it's a London thing.   He is obviously a knob
but a happy one   and that   it seems to me
is the important   though not localisable   thing.

Carolina

After Frank Zappa, George Gershwin, The Raconteurs, Counting Crows, Claudia
Church, Alabama, Bucky Covington, Sheryl Crow, Brand New, Mary Black, James
Taylor, Jo Dee Messina and Josh Turner

Having always thought, someday, I'd burn that bed
I left with nothing but a cold bologna sandwich
a borrowed suit, pockets full of dust and found myself

a thousand miles away, amongst the mountain dew
and, later, amongst smokey mountain eyes
in a crowded back-room, where every look was thrown

like a knife and I thought the game was over, but
sitting on three queens I made a train at sunrise.
That night, I swallowed liquor and a lighter

and found her like moonlight falling on a bed.
I could have swore her hair was made of rayon
and when we kissed she tasted like a loaded gun.

The sound of bluegrass and southern words
wove their ways to an old Sandlapper tune
between Palmetto trees and Geese in flight.

Wearing a Milton-Bradley crayon, she whispered
something warm about the height of cotton,

asked if I could feel the moon shine

and beneath the silver sun I asked her
what she'd say to setting out for getting lost.
She sent me to the milkman, looking for the truth.

Merlin Grey

The varieties of household paint proliferate;
Crown's glosses, mattes and silks spill over,
fill the book I find between Catullus

and Celan. Donaghy and Donne
flank a Dulux brochure. And yes
I'm trying to show how well-read I am.

Or to cite a line between compulsion
and abandon – the just-off alphabetical
 I've whittled to a totem – a prop

 with which to strut the bounds
of personality. *Contradiction in coherence
expresses the force of desire*, apparently.

Re:

As soup made Eliot think of Spinoza
and *she* made Donne think of compasses
drummers drumming bring to mind αλήθεια

and how, for the Greeks, truth was uncoveredness;
drummers true drummers only by their drumming,
tangled thighs the criterion of lovers.

And my point, true love, is that I've been thinking
and don't think I can love someone who struggles
with the latent – flowers well before blooming –

whose gifts must, without fail, be spectacles
and never a package of crepe paper and dirt
which, water added, might turn mud or vegetables:

artichokes, small but incontrovertibly *vert*;
the promise of a purple patch next year.

Rosenmontag

In Munich   the trams still run   though snow hunkers
beside the tracks   and each building looks beyond

repair   baying to buckle   onto the *platz*.
There   we are all   varying degrees of drunk

off steins of beer   or cartons   of sweet wine
shared in swigs.   Sarah bemoans a groper.

Locals hunker to a doorstep   one drags a girl
towards him.   She dribbles sweet   *Ich liebe Dich*

and means it.   I mean   she's not just cooing
through that mist   of exhaled booze   and snow

sublimandum under a crowd's foot.   I can't set
meaning to her words   but feel it   how she intones

herself to him   presses each sound   as a tender fact
that will not be solicited.   Sarah is pressed against me.

JAMES WILKES

Two Review Poems

Linda Hadley and Edwin Hak, *6 London Fountains* **(Canterbury: Panda Press, 2008), 8pp.**

One ragged sheet they complicate down, a small hand-inked dribbler, of slit and fold and press within the pages. 13 spumante pencils, the central higher than the rest.

The "rational fountain", bisected by the shadows of financial courts, turns water to a fabric draped unwrinkled over marble slabs. But a wobble turns a ravel, and it seams.

The dampened husk and scaffold of a civic flow: the blocked stone fountain gathers surplus, of material, of rainspots, in the park.

Robert Steinbeck, *The Leaping Pebble: a Philosophical Novel*, **ed. and foreword by James Lewes, Gertrude Felix and Ray Harms (Edinburgh: Stott Books, 2002), 198pp.**

Speculative biomedical ethics meets dancehall reverie in this elegant folio reprint of the hard-to-find private press original (1908). Editorial cuts by Lewes et al. are largely faithful to the author's intent, unlike Kendal's bowdlerising excisions of 1934 (though see Selene Camphor, 'Kendal, Steinbeck et le problème de proprioception' in *Études baltiques* 65 for an alternative view). Relocating the scene of the ambiguous sexual encounter from Behlersee (Schleswig-Holstein) to Battersea (Wandsworth) is an interesting move, though it does make the appearance of the famous black stork rather anomalous.

For anyone with even the slightest interest in whether the neural correlates of consciousness might be understood via a bedsheet tied to broomhandles on which coloured images flurry, settle, detach like film of ashes, this is a must. Otherwise wait for the stage adaptation. If chatroom gossip is correct, this will be set in Thessaloniki circa 2030, and opens with Ludwig (Robert Redford) attempting to fence DNA stolen from a medieval saint's fingerbone.

Two theatrical branches of the Muse's vine which are legitimate topics of poetry

Bike Couriers

A bike couriers' soirée might happen in an abandoned multi-storey with fluorescent tube lights propped in corners, cans of iced beer sold from a wheelbarrow and a choice of hard trance or the music of falling concrete. Post-industrial minimalism may be démodé but they do it with flair.

Also bike couriers are interesting because they shuttle desirable items through smog and danger. Such as contracts, deeds of sale, blackmail demands, blood samples, gigs of unrefined data, fashion accessories, sandwiches, and high-res satellite shots of factories in Guangdong.

These piratical nomads service capitalism on the cheap risking bodily injury in the forced spaces between membranes. Power needs differential (see watermills, synapses etc.) and if two membranes touch all information disastrously finds its level and is called a merger.

So bike couriers are like butchers or meat packers, whose jobs are also quite dangerous and who are trusted despite appearances. Not hypocrites, they confront complicity in keeping the boundaries cruel and functional. But for a poet what bike couriers have over butchers is a sense of style.

Heavy red twill ripped off at the knee. Bike oil, sweat and headphones, bleach and clippers, ornament the brain case. The heavy hardened links the waist. The tweaked-out racers, oilskin bags and radio static blur. Who would not want to glamorise these fast people?

Fireworks

Their saltpetre trajectories remind us that leisure and war are spun from the same material and maths. And when they go off the flat sky gains depth and artifice for the duration they expand.

They are liked by small children though not by pets. And indeed, children don't neglect to write poems about them. This tendency creeps in with adulthood and is a mistake. Up, up up! Tris! Tris! Bang!

They sketch a ghostly commons from incandescent specks. It is our chemical weather, drifting this way and that, baroque mixture of earth and breath. Even for a private celebration, they are sent up over the wall.

Solitary and emulsified by rain, or packed in so the scent of cordite pricks each nostril. No-one trusts them, the claim to pure expenditure and nothing back, the way they compel a crowd to crane upwards.

from Venus & Other Noises

Terrene to coalesce a pretty terror
Parties weights sycophant moreover
Ulterior the onerous needle svelte
Drawers us two-dream dusk drag
Wood's verdant memory gone

Unsought all import quarantine claw
Queue you dogs of Venus bawd
If not fjord love flock name
Nested penurious teak streams
Tracks stalk clustered bridges

That is to state the sunflower skeleton
Had her designs on the speed of the tarmac
Is the sprack of my love, I spoken so ardent
I malvine walls to westward join

Though if in momentum grew these rocks?
What then, to what election do I vote?
Multidimensional oxen yoke - Gravity joke

Black phoneme rooks birth loss

The cloud sod sad, to be glad without hope
Or hopes return, to get on your optic nerve
Hung as gristle between bird beak
Your orbit gaze, frame & steam
When do we speak?

So long after acid veil drops heaven
Accelerated water & Absented lava flow
Is this hell for why do you call me love?
To keep my inferior orbit, where we tremor

You used to send me phoneme skulls
Yet now I gleam for Lovers
Amongst the satellites and adverts
To hear my name of lust

Half Flesh - Half sulphuric stone
Umbrella night you remonstrated
For empathy but sedimented London
Or the intercoporeality will

Ease her passing
So speak this rock awake
Possible coiling as earth
As in the horrid of the heavens

from Source

A hyperlinked Walk Through 12 Battersea Bomb Sites

Crossing onto Cumberland Street, the tall grey
Clock had rotated the earth's axis without
Warning had jumped thirty-five minutes
Into white future, his limbs out of proportion pixilated
Felt leaden, statues of bronze bone, megalithic
Knee joints set out on granite plinths
Onto Clarendon St, and right onto Winchester, a street play
Scheme burrowed underground into the centre of the explosion.
He kicked through the reference ruin - bombsite hyperlinked into
            Bombsite
On Claverton Street. By-words.
That detach and meander on cords.
On Lupus Street he imagined the city as a calcareous skeleton
Secreted by certain marine Polyps
Reddish ornamentations forming
Reefs, and islands, woven together by fibre
Optic tendrils, very beautiful, and very dead.

Utopian dreams of glass are scoffed at
By running beans ridiculously plump
Tomatoes burgeoning red with sale.

Past the world-house across Douglass Street
And back, being careful not to be seen
Crouching behind a tarpaulin shed
And the drills everywhere
Twenty-one coiled and rasping bores, digging
Always digging, twenty-one gravel-hoovers, crunched
Up in noise
Crabbed for a photograph
In agony he passed out in the street.

Heavy static stoic welders arc upon the stroke
Of four horrendous garbled java slat to flash dance
Hacker acumen telepathic sagacious spine poetics
Of the dark: Multiple signals. All around. Closing -

from Portmanteaux

WORK: what entropic value sinks between
Kelly Rowland's chiffon toile chain
gang trudge treadwheel or Calvinist ethics
Severance package dished up T.V dinner

Anchor weights to the letter house -
Before rent in our own flesh
Attrition applies across dispersal
The black wood scowls and bleeds

Unionised bodies ingrown as toenails
Pullulating pulchritudinous made
Outcast flies catch death in process
*& Invitation they lick the concrete cracks

Subcontracted language gags on staves
Light-pink sunlight hues dapple Stansted
Harvest planes layoff
Sack the symmetrical land
Watch blue rape

Translation is obfuscation in labour
Lawfully wed and two croppy clusters kiss
Yeah, I heard it God squats in this house
Man! On the third day the open plan office

Apprentice figures whelm and soy
Tawny toys the coteries of saturated fats
She's singing, "d-do it baby get it don't come
Around if you gonna let me down you gotta
Get it all the way in I wanna see you work"

from Wave (Histories of the Kursk)

Ultraviolet Radiation

Visions of bees circle your breath
As their dark amber glows hotter

At the end they all see the blue
Orbed sun the disconsolate plumage

Seared and moody in thick black
Light as phoenix transactions

Permit your travel into sad closeted
Abstraction the metonymic paper

Perhaps all we should do is the tail wag
The critical dances of being

Which turns flowers into runways
Of departure circular arrival at the petal

Picked clocks convulse the navigated sun
Sunk and salty and your pumped blood boils

When quickly removed from pressure
Those jammed hatches and sown pockets

That seam to confirm the silence or noise
When streptococcal complaints in bubbles

Stop so what is a Micro-photolithographic
Poetics of socio-circuit boards and market Networks

I want to kiss each inch the man said
Diving through manoeuvred practices

To see in silicone his furrowed hand
Struggling to fill the ballast tanks

Showing that familial relations
Are spectrum relations and metallic

Reverberations on dismantled hulls
Or skulls vaporized in the bleak of black.

Biographical notes

JAY BERNARD was born in London in 1988. Her poetry has appeared in *Poetry London*, *The Guardian* and *The Independent*, and performed on Radio 4's The Green Room and Radio 3's The Verb as well as at Trafalgar Square and on the Culture Show. She won the London Respect Slam in 2004 and in 2005 was selected as a Foyle Young Poet of the Year. Her debut, *Your Sign is Cuckoo, Girl* (Tall Lighthouse, 2008), was selected as a PBS pamphlet choice.

CAROLINE BIRD was born in London in 1986. She is the author of *Looking Through Letterboxes* and *Trouble Came to the Turnip* (both Carcanet). Caroline has won an Eric Gregory award and was a Foyle Young Poet Of the Year twice; her recent collection was shortlisted for the Dylan Thomas Prize 2008. She has read at the Royal Festival Hall and Manchester, Cheltenham and Ledbury literature festivals. She is currently studying English at Oxford University.

BEN BOREK was born in Camberwell in 1980. He graduated from The University of East Anglia Creative Writing MA in 2004. His novel in verse, *Donjong Heights*, was published last year by Egg Box Publishing. His poems have appeared in various magazines and anthologies and he has read his work all over Britain, in Europe and on BBC Radio. He lives in London and is currently working on his second book.

SIDDHARTHA BOSE was born in 1979, raised in Bombay and Calcutta, and lived for seven years in the United States. A trained actor and filmmaker, his poetry has appeared in *The Wolf, Tears in the Fence, Fulcrum, Eclectica* and *Alhamra Literary Review*, and is anthologized in *Voice Recognition: 21 Poets for the 21st Century* (Bloodaxe, 2009). He currently lives in London and is completing a PhD on the Grotesque at Queen Mary, University of London.

TOM CHIVERS was born in 1983 in South London. A writer, editor and promoter of poetry, his publications include *The Terrors* (Nine Arches Press, 2009) and *How To Build A City* (Salt Publishing, 2009). A winner of the inaugural Crashaw Prize, he is Associate Editor of *Tears in the Fence*, was Poet in Residence at The Bishopsgate Institute, London, and has appeared on BBC Radio 3 and 4. Tom is Director of Penned in the Margins and Co-Director of London Word Festival.

SWITHUN COOPER was born in 1983 and graduated from the Warwick Writing Programme. He lives in London. Swithun's creative work has appeared in magazines including *Acumen*, *The London Magazine* and *PN Review*. In his spare time he puts on events with the feminist collective Manifesta.

ALEX DAVIES was born in 1984 and lives in Wigan. He co-runs the Openned reading series and website in London and co-founded The Other Room series in Manchester. His work has been published in *veer off* (Veer Books, 2008) and *Past Simple*. Extracts of his work, including an audio performance of a section of his latest work LONDONSTONE, can be found at openned.com

INUA ELLAMS was born in 1984 in Nigeria and lives in London. He is a Word & Graphic Artist who constantly strives to merge the two disciplines. His work in both fields is known for its rich imagery and attention to detail. Inua is influenced equally by classic literature and hip-hop culture; his poetry fuses archaic language and sentence structure with contemporary diction, loose rhythm and rhyme. His pamphlet *Thirteen Fairy Negro Tales* was published by Flipped Eye in 2005.

LAURA FORMAN was born in Basingstoke in 1979, educated at Cambridge and lives in South London. Her poetry has been published in various magazines and the anthology *Generation Txt*. She was recently commissioned by Galaxy Chocolate. Laura works as the writer at Elmwood London, a design agency based in Soho. The space is more like a bar than an office so Laura programmes and hosts a quarterly poetry night there called SoPo. She occasionally reviews pop music and fiction for *The Financial Times*.

WAYNE HOLLOWAY-SMITH was born in 1979. He is currently a student of creative writing at Brunel University. His poems have been published in *The Wolf, Rising, Pen Pusher* and *Life Lines 2: Poets for Oxfam*. His short story, *Hyperpsychoreality Syndrome*, was released as an audiobook by BBC New Writing. His pocket book of poetry is forthcoming from Donut Press.

CHRISTOPHER HORTON was born in 1978 and lives in London. His poems have been published (or are forthcoming) in *Iota, Dream Catcher, Other Poetry, The Wolf, Magma, Fuselit, Ambit, Stand* and *City Lighthouse* (Tall Lighthouse). Co-host of East Words at Museum in Docklands, Christopher was commended in the 2008 National Poetry Competition.

KIRSTEN IRVING was born in 1983 in a Lincolnshire village so small it doesn't even have its own Wikipedia entry. She is the submissions editor of *Fuselit* magazine and her writing has appeared in a variety of publications, including *Rising, Shakespeare's Monkeys, Toad in Mud* and *Mimesis*. She is currently putting together her first pamphlet, maintaining the facade of naturally pillar box hair and doing her Rickenbacker justice.

ANNIE KATCHINSKA was born in Moscow in 1990 and has lived in London for most of her life. She won a Foyle Young Poet of the Year award in 2006 and came second in the Christopher Tower Poetry Competition in 2007. Her poems have appeared in *Magma* and *Mimesis* and she has performed at New Blood at the Poetry Café. Annie is currently in the middle of a Classics degree at Cambridge.

AMY KEY was born in Dover in 1978. She grew up in Kent and Tyneside and has lived and worked in London since 2001. She co-organises The Shuffle reading series and edited *The Shuffle Anthology 2007-2008*. Her poetry has been published in *Magma*, *South Bank Poetry*, *Smiths Knoll* and *Rising*. Her first pamphlet, *instead of stars*, was published by Tall Lighthouse in 2009 as part of their Pilot series.

CHRIS MCCABE was born in Liverpool in 1977. His work has appeared in magazines including *Magma* and *Poetry Review* and he has published two collections with Salt – *The Hutton Inquiry* (2005) and *Zeppelins* (2009). He has discussed and read his poetry on BBC World Service, featured a poem on the Oxfam CD *Lifelines* and performs his work regularly. Chris works as Joint Librarian of The Poetry Library and lives in Dagenham with his wife and son.

MARIANNE MUNK was born in 1982 and spent the early part of her life in South Africa. She's lived in the UK since 1997, and London since 2004. Her pamphlets include *Madam, I'm Damaged* (Barque, 1998); *Scrum in the Cum* (yt communication, 2007); *I Capture the Cold Sore* (Critical Documents, 2007); and *Beaten by Chastisement* (Veer Books, 2008). A finance secretary by day, by night she just puts the "factotum" in fuck totem or whatevs.

HOLLY PESTER was born in 1982. She uses the materiality of speech to compose performance-driven works that experiment playfully with semantic meaning and identity. She has recently completed a Masters in Creative and Critical Writing and is preparing a PhD in sound poetry and transmedia poetics. She has previously collaborated with poets James Wilkes and Abigail Oborne, and with a composer from Guildhall School of Music and Drama.

HEATHER PHILLIPSON was born in London in 1978. She works as a professional artist and regularly exhibits nationally and internationally. She was awarded the Michael Donaghy Poetry Prize in 2007, an Eric Gregory Award and a commendation in the Troubadour Poetry Prize in 2008, and a Faber New Poets Award in 2009. She has a pamphlet forthcoming from Faber and Faber.

NICK POTAMITIS was born in 1975 and grew up in North London. His poems have appeared in *Shearsman* and the *Openned Anthology*. 'anti-gravity belt projects' first appeared in Issue One of *Axolotl*. His collection *N.* was published by Perdika Press in 2006.

IMOGEN ROBERTSON was born in Darlington in 1973. She is a TV, film and radio director and her first novel, *Instruments of Darkness*, is published by Headline in 2009. She was commended in the National Poetry Competition 2005. She has lived in London since 1997, staying as near to the Thames as possible at all times.

JACOB SAM-LA ROSE was born in 1976. His pamphlet *Communion* was selected for a Poetry Book Society award in 2006. He is Artistic Director of the London Teenage Poetry SLAM, Editor-in-Chief of Metaroar.com, and an editor for Flipped Eye Press. Jacob facilitates a range of literature-in-education, creative writing and spoken word programmes for schools, arts centres and other institutions around the world.

ASHNA SARKAR was born in 1992 in London to two immanently divorcing social workers. A young writer with more eyeliner than sense, Ashna's poetry takes you on a guided tour from Camden Lock to the Surrey Downs, charting the perils of adolescence. She was dubbed 'Britain's hippest young Asian poet' by Roddy Lumsden.

JON STONE was born in 1983. His writing has appeared in *The Wolf, Mimesis, Nth-position* and *Rising*. He is production editor of *Fuselit*. Jon lives in Whitechapel and works as a transcript editor in London's courts and arbitration centres.

BARNABY TIDMAN was born in 1986 and lives in London. He is interested in de-mystification/mystification, sonic fiction, subconscious poetics, William Burroughs, and cinema. He is wrapping up the first issue of his new magazine *Summer Scars*, which will be available in print and download from April 2009 (summerscars.com).

AHREN WARNER was born in 1986. His poems and the occasional review have appeared in *Poetry Review, Magma, The Wolf* and others. His work is forthcoming in the Bloodaxe anthologies *Voice Recognition: 21 Poets for the 21st Century* and *Identity Parade: New British and Irish Poets*. Ahren recently received an Arts Council England Award and is working towards his first collection. He is currently studying for an MA in Critical Methodologies. He lives in Hackney.

JAMES WILKES was born in Poole, Dorset in 1980. He is in his first year of a PhD at the London Consortium. His poetry has been published in various places including *Tears in the Fence, Intercapillary Space*, The Archive of the Now, *Great Works* and *Generation Txt*. He reviews contemporary art, writes for radio and theatre, and is currently working on a radio drama project about brain imaging. See renscombepress.co.uk

STEVE WILLEY was born in 1984. He lives in Whitechapel and co-runs Openned (openned.com). His work is published or forthcoming in *veer off* (Veer Books, 2008), *Stimulus Respond, Onedit 11, Past Simple, Klatch* and *Axolotl 3*. His hand-made accordion book *Wave: (Histories of the Kursk)* has been archived by the British Library; *Venus & Other Noises* is published by Yt Communication in 2009. He is undertaking a collaborative PhD at Queen Mary entitled 'British Poetry and Performance 1960-2008'.